PAINTING ON THE
Wild Side!

Sharon Stansifer CDA

NORTH LIGHT BOOKS

CINCINNATI, OHIO

www.artistsnetwork.com

ABOUT THE AUTHOR

Sharon Stansifer CDA was born in Memphis, Tennessee, but was raised a California girl. She has always loved creating art in all forms, from cartooning and working in pastels, oils and acrylics, to making graphite sketches of abstract form. Her current artwork focuses on wildlife and strokework.

Sharon became involved in the decorative art style of painting in 1986 and began teaching in 1991. She has received her CDA certification from the Society of Decorative Artists and passed her Master Decorative Artist Stroke exam in 1999.

Currently living in southern California, Sharon has been married to husband, Laurie, for 23 years, and they have two sons, Ryan, age 19, and Kyle, 16. Her previous North Light book was *The Complete Book of Basic Brushstrokes for Decorative Painters*.

Other fine North Light Books are available from your local bookstore, art supply store or direct from the publisher.

05 04 03 02   5 4 3 2

Library of Congress Cataloging-in-Publication Data

Stansifer, Sharon
    Painting on the wild side! / by Sharon Stansifer
      p. cm.
    Includes index.
    ISBN 1-58180-159-9 (pb : alk. paper)
      1. Wildlife painting--Technique. I. Title.

ND1380 .S7 2001
751.45'432--dc21   2001030110

Editor: Christine Doyle
Production Coordinator: Kristen D. Heller
Cover Design: Stephanie Strang
Interior Design: Joanna Detz
Layout Artist: Kathy Bergstrom
Photographer: Christine Polomsky

METRIC CONVERSION CHART

to convert	to	multiply by
Inches	Centimeters	2.54
Centimeters	Inches	0.4
Feet	Centimeters	30.5
Centimeters	Feet	0.03
Yards	Meters	0.9
Meters	Yards	1.1
Sq. Inches	Sq. Centimeters	6.45
Sq. Centimeters	Sq. Inches	0.16
Sq. Feet	Sq. Meters	0.09
Sq. Meters	Sq. Feet	10.8
Sq. Yards	Sq. Meters	0.8
Sq. Meters	Sq. Yards	1.2
Pounds	Kilograms	0.45
Kilograms	Pounds	2.2
Ounces	Grams	28.4
Grams	Ounces	0.04

DEDICATION

To the men in my life.

This book is dedicated first of all to my dad, Keith Tieszen, for all the hard work and effort you put into me. And yes, I know I was a handful, and still you were and are a great father! I'm so appreciative to you for all your love and support.

Many people have inspired me in my artwork over the last several years, but it was my dad who inspired me to paint my first piece of wildlife. My mom's house was filled with many Victorian-style floral paintings that she so loves and inspires, so I figured it was time to paint something just for my dad. Boy, did that open an entirely new world for me—I fell in love with all the fur and feathers. I have been enthralled by it ever since. Thanks dad, for the idea and inspiration.

To my three boys: my husband, Laurie, and sons, Ryan and Kyle. I hope you are enjoying the new decor in our home that includes a more masculine touch from all these wildlife paintings.

To all the boys, big and small, who are tired of being surrounded by all the flowers and "fluffy, cutesie" stuff painted by the decorative-painting loved ones in their lives—finally you can enjoy something a little more on the wild side!

ACKNOWLEDGMENTS

Thank you so much to Janet Cattolica for helping (and pushing) me any and every time I needed it (which was often). You have been such a good friend and have been more help than I could ever make you know. Thank you!

To my family, my husband, Laurie, and sons, Kyle and Ryan. For all you endured during the enormous time it took to put a book like this together, I thank you. You have been so supportive. May it come back to bless us as a family and as individuals.

To my students, you are the best. No teacher could be more blessed with more wonderful and loyal students. Thank you so much for all your support and love. I can only pray that I have touched your lives in a way you will always carry with you and that all your future paintings will show it. Thank you for being my willing "guinea pigs" over and over again! I love you!

Thank you to all the wonderful suppliers for this book: Delta, Daler-Rowney, Viking Woodcrafts and Valhalla. Your support helps make it possible for me to create and inspire my students.

And of course, thank you to my editors at North Light Books: Christine Doyle, Kathy Kipp, Greg Albert and David Lewis (thanks for finding me). Also to my photographer, Christine Polomsky, who makes eight-hour photo shoot days seem not so long!

TABLE OF CONTENTS

INTRODUCTION

I find the world of animals amazing, from the majestic lions, tigers and bears (oh my!), to smaller critters like chipmunks and song birds. Sometimes I turn on the Animal Planet channel and watch it for hours! Animals can be cute and cuddly as well as awesome. Seeing animals in their natural habitat is the best of all.

Painting animals both big and small can be very rewarding. There is just something about the amazing array of colors and textures—they seem unending. With every animal I paint, I feel I have captured something special in their fur, feathers, colors or eyes. Then I see a new subject and I realize there is still so much more!

Painting is the perfect way to "hunt and capture" animals: By painting them you can display them in all their beauty, the adventure need never end, and you can keep them safe for all the world to see. Endangered species are becoming special favorites of mine. It is unimaginable that some of these animals are so few in number and that their very survival is at risk. Wildlife artwork can be a great way to raise awareness on their behalf.

Although wildlife painting may seem different from other decorative painting subjects, like roses or fresh cherries, the trick is to go step by step and focus on what can make your painting special. Learning and practicing the techniques used in this book to create the different textures of fur, the glow of wild eyes, and the detail of a bird's feathers can make you a better painter overall. Skills like brush control are key in all types of painting—soon you will begin to see your brush dance as you create your favorite subjects.

Over my years of teaching painting, I have found that the personality of the painter is often expressed in the finished painting. Several people can paint the same design, and each finished piece will look different. This is a *good* thing—it is one way we can each creatively express ourselves. So don't be discouraged if your pieces don't turn out exactly like the ones in this book— your paintings are uniquely yours!

The world would be a very different place indeed without our wonderful furred and feathered friends. May we be blessed enough to never see that day! There is an almost unlimited supply of beautiful animals throughout the world waiting to be discovered. I hope this book gets you hooked on painting wildlife and that you love every feather and tuft of fur you paint!

May your future be filled with beautiful paintings.

Sharon Stansifer, CDA

CHAPTER ONE

materials

Fabric Master liner

Fabric Master
angle scrubber

Fabric Master
round scrubber

Fabric Master
round basecoater

Fabric Master
flat basecoater

Expression
flat wash

AquaTip
oval wash

Expression
angle shader

Expression wash

Expression
chisel blender

Expression round

Expression round

Expression liner

BRUSHES
Robert Simmons
Expression Brushes

Artist-quality brushes will make all the difference in the process and outcome of your paintings. The Robert Simmons Expression line of brushes is perfect for a consistent quality. The Golden Taklon hairs hold their shape well, and they put up with all the abuse I give them and still perform excellently. The handles are the best! They are larger in diameter than most, tremendously reducing wrist and hand fatigue when painting for any length of time. This is very noticeable for anyone with wrist problems like mine. After having wrist surgery a few years ago, I am always on the lookout for products that can help decrease pain and discomfort and increase the length of time I can continue to paint. These brushes meet those needs beautifully.

Robert Simmons
AquaTip Brushes

These also have the larger handles and perform beautifully as the larger ovals (or filberts) I need.

Robert Simmons
Decorator Stencil Brushes

These brushes have the perfect "bounce" to their bristles. They are great for stencilling, drybrushing and creating a variety of faux finishes.

Robert Simmons Fabric Master

The fabric brushes have stiffer bristles in order to push the paint into the weave of the fabric. They hold up to the scrubbing motion that may be needed to get the definition of the pattern into the fabric.

Loew-Cornell Filbert Rake

The LaCorneille Golden Taklon 7520 ¼-inch (6mm) filbert rake is the brush I have used throughout this book to create the beautifully realistic fur. It is like using one hundred liner brushes to get all those natural hairs in every stroke. Once you learn to use this brush you will make sure to always have one handy any time you need to paint fur or hair.

Loew-Cornell ¼-inch
(6mm) filbert rake
and 18/0 short liner

Loew-Cornell 18/0 Short Liner

The LaCorneille Golden Taklon 7350 18/0 short liner is the perfect brush for complete control in tiny areas and when painting lines and lashes— and always for your signature.

PAINTS

Delta Bottled Acrylics

Delta paints have the widest range of colors currently available. They have a wonderful selection of warm and rich natural colors that make it easier to create the beauty of animals. The consistency and coverage of the paints is great and they're easy to work with.

Delta Fabric Dyes

I really enjoy working with these paints. Delta has a beautiful array of fabric colors in regular, shimmering and glitter paints. Try any of the patterns in this book on fabric and wear your artwork. It is easy to get the texture of the animal because the fabric already provides the texture! Wildlife fabric prints are very popular and make a beautiful statement about the person wearing them! I have given instructions on converting one of the designs in this book, the cardinal in project two, to the fabric dyes.

BASIC SUPPLIES

- Loew-Cornell Brush Tub II (384)
- Black, gray and white graphite paper
- Tack cloth to remove wood dust

- Sanding pads, 300- and 600-grit
- Magic Rub eraser
- Paper towels. Use high-quality regular paper towels or shop towels.
- Cotton swabs. The cheaper ones work best.
- Stylus for transferring patterns
- Tracing paper
- Palette paper for acrylic paints
- Delta Wood Sealer. Apply to raw wood before painting for a smoother overall finished painting.
- Delta Brush Cleaner, my preference
- Dry-It Board. This allows air to move all around your pieces as you seal and basecoat them and prevents marks.
- Ultra-fine permanent marker
- Low-tack blue painter's tape or 3M Scotch Magic Tape
- Delta Matte Interior Spray Varnish. This is a low-odor product that doesn't affect my allergies.
- Delta Matte Interior Varnish
- Chalk pencils, white and gray, or a soapstone

FAUX FINISHING MATERIALS

- Delta Fabric Gel Medium. Mix with fabric dyes to make it easier for the paints to move and penetrate the fabric.
- Delta Gel Stain Medium. Mix with regular Delta paints to create transparent stains and antiquing effects.

- Delta Gel Blending Medium. Mix with Delta paints to extend (or slow) the drying time for easier blending.
- Delta Crackle Medium. Layering this product between coats of paint produces natural-looking cracks for wood and rocks.
- Delta Cherished Memories Stencil Sponges for blending paint.
- Upholstery foam wedges, coarse-cut squares of dense foam for a rougher appearance when blending paint.
- 2-inch (51mm) foam brush for rough basecoating or slip-slapping background colors together.
- Fuzz-free cotton balls. Just use a drugstore bagged brand marked "fuzz-free" so they don't shed.
- 12-inch (30cm) see-through ruler, for marking edges and borders.
- Gold leafing, thin sheets of gold, torn to create a rich, old-world effect.
- Gold leafing adhesive, a tacky adhesive that doesn't completely dry; the gold leafing goes on top of the adhesive.

CHAPTER TWO

techniques

CREATING REALISTIC FUR AND FEATHERS

Creating realistic-looking fur and feathers isn't hard, you just need to keep in mind a few tips and techniques. First I'll discuss the most important things to remember when painting fur—directional flow and natural unevenness—then I'll describe the actual techniques for painting soft, full fur, including color weaving.

DIRECTIONAL FLOW

Included with each project in this book is a directional flow diagram. This diagram is an outline of the animal with arrows drawn on it to show the direction the fur would grow. The fur direction gives the animal shape and dimension. For example, if you do not give a slight arch to the fur as it flows around the sides of an animal's head, the head will not have dimension (it will look flat). It is important to think about the fur direction of each part of the animal you are working on. The direction will change as you move throughout your painting. Continually stop yourself as you are painting and check the directional flow diagram, making adjustments as needed.

NATURAL UNEVENNESS

Things in nature have a randomness to their appearance. Even the two sides of a person's face are not exactly the same! Try not to make the fur too perfect. For example, do not start and stop the fur colors exactly in the same place, or pull the fur with such consistency that the hairs of the fur look all the same.

To achieve this "natural unevenness," vary the pressure applied to the brush throughout the animal. Use the flat of the brush at times and the chisel at others. This will make some thin hairs, some thick hairs and some tufts.

MIXING THE PAINT AND LOADING THE BRUSH

The strokes you make when you paint fur and feathers are important, but before you start painting, you need to pay particular attention to the consistency of the paint you use, your brushes, and the way you load the brush.

In order to create a stroke that flows properly off the brush, the paint needs to be mixed with water to an inklike consistency. Follow the instructions on the opposite page for mixing the paint to the consistency of ink. Use this same mix of water and paint for your linework as well.

For painting the fur strokes, I have found two different brushes that work well: Loew-Cornell's filbert rake and a round brush. For my tinier animals I prefer the round brush; for the others, I work with the filbert rake.

Once you have selected the brush for the animal, or area of the animal, you are painting, follow the instructions on page 12 for loading the brush. This technique for loading the brush separates the bristles, so that each stroke you make looks like a dozen strokes made by a liner brush. You may not need to load the brush like this when you basecoat the fur and feathers (see individual projects for instructions), but you will need to load the brush this way each time you paint the light detail strokes on the birds and the color weaving on the animals.

Brushing-mixing for an Inklike Consistency

1 Put equal amounts of paint and water on your palette.

2 Begin to mix the paint and water with the brush.

3 Continue mixing until the puddle comes to an even, inky consistency.

4 Blot the brush on a dry paper towel by putting pressure on the ferrule and pulling until all the extra paint mixture soaks out of the brush.

5 Turn the brush over and repeat on the other side.

LOADING A LINER BRUSH FOR LINEWORK

1 Lay the liner brush in the edge of the puddle of thinned paint (mixed as described at left) and apply pressure.

2 Pull the brush out from the puddle, rolling the brush in your fingers as you pull.

3 This creates a nice pointed end to the liner, which works well for painting whiskers, feather detail or signing your name to the finished piece.

Loading a Filbert Rake Brush for Fur

1 Keeping the handle straight up and down, place the brush into the puddle, applying full pressure to the brush.

2 Pull the brush out of the puddle into a clean area on your palette paper.

3 While maintaining pressure on the brush, twist the handle one way to begin to splay out the bristles.

Tip

When painting fur always turn the piece so that you are pulling the strokes toward yourself. Set the brush down at the base of the fur and pull toward the tips of the hairs. The base of a hair is thicker, gradually getting thinner as it reaches the tip.

4 Twist the handle the other way so the bristles are fully and evenly splayed.

5 This method of loading the brush separates bristles so you can create many individual hairs with one stroke.

Loading a Round or Liner Brush for Fur and Feathers

  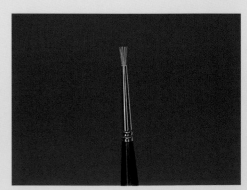

1 Thin the paint with water to an inky consistency as described on page 11.

2 Blot your brush with a dry paper towel. Dip the brush in the thinned paint and pull it out a bit. Splay the bristles first in one direction, then the other to form a half circle.

3 The bristles are now separated and the strokes made with the brush will be feathery, like the many individual hairs of a rake brush. Use these smaller brushes in small areas, like on the wings of a bird or the face of a squirrel.

COLOR WEAVING

"Color weaving" is what I call the technique I use to create the soft density of realistic fur. It really is the key. Often when people paint animal fur it looks very coarse and unrealistic because the fur strokes are just sitting on top of each other. When you color weave, you use delicate strokes to paint hairlike lines of all the different colors of fur; these strokes make the fur look soft and they serve to lessen the harshness between different colors of fur. Color weaving is the difference between a wildlife painting that looks good and one that looks lifelike.

After you have basecoated the fur with rough fur strokes, you are ready to color weave. When weaving the fur, use your filbert rake brush to mix your paints with water to an inklike consistency (as described on page 11) so that the paint flows properly off the hairs of the brush. Load the filbert as described on page 12.

To color weave, start with your brush loaded with any of the basecoat colors and place the brush on an area painted with that color. Apply a light amount of pressure on the brush and release as you stroke into the fur color next to the one in which you started. While pulling the fur in this manner, it is very important to have all the pressure off the brush at the end of the stroke so that the hairs are increasingly fine. This will help give the appearance that some hairs go under others. The ends of the hairs that do show are very tapered.

Continue pulling strokes into neighboring color with a very light touch. Use all the basecoat colors, and cover smaller and smaller areas so that every color used shows. (See project five for more instructions for color weaving.)

Color weaving is a time-consuming process, but it does make all the difference in a wildlife painting. The more you weave the fur, the denser it will appear, like a thick winter coat. If you desire a more summer coat appearance, repeat the color-weaving steps fewer times.

First basecoat the animal, following the directional flow diagram. All the colors that will be used in the fur have been added at this point. The filbert rake is used to basecoat the tiger's stripes, and for all but the first layers, the paint is thinned and the brush is loaded as described previously. But because you are basecoating, the strokes are coarse and not as light and fine as they will be for color weaving.

To color weave, load the filbert rake with thinned paint, as described previously, and pull light strokes from the base color into the neighboring color. Pull the color into the neighbor on the other side as well.

Repeat for all the basecoat colors, pulling light strokes into the neighboring colors.

In this image, the color weaving is complete. Notice how much softer the fur on the cheeks and chest look—you almost want to reach out and touch it!

Complete instructions for color weaving begin on page 72 in project five.

Winter Morning Blue Jay

On a cold winter morning the beautiful blue jay stays perfectly warm with his well-groomed feathers. The markings on the blue jay are so striking—they make him a treat to admire and paint.

On this piece, the faux-finished background gives the same appearance as a soft-focus lens in photography: blurring the flowers, leaves and sky while keeping the blue jay and his snowy perch in sharp focus. Repeating the snowy branch and berries around the blue jay creates a beautiful yet nondistracting frame to keep the viewer's eye on the bird.

MATERIALS

SURFACE

9½" (24cm) octagonal plate from Viking Woodcrafts, Inc. (Alternate surface: 6" [15cm] punch tin with lid from Viking Woodcrafts, Inc. shown on page 14)

BRUSHES

Robert Simmons Expression
no. 0 script liner
no. 0 round
no. 1 round
no. 3 round
⅛" (3mm) angle shader
¼" (6mm) angle shader
1" (25mm) flat

Robert Simmons AquaTip
¾" (19mm) oval wash

Loew-Cornell
18/0 short liner

ADDITIONAL SUPPLIES

Delta Cherished Memories
    Stencil Sponges
Delta Matte Interior Spray Varnish
gray graphite paper
Delta Matte Interior Varnish

DELTA CERAMCOAT ACRYLICS

Ocean Reef Blue | Blue Jay | Periwinkle Blue | Lavender Lace

Chambray Blue | Dolphin Grey | Green Sea | Pine Green

Black | Blueberry | Brown Velvet | Chocolate Cherry

Opaque Red | Lilac | Ice Storm Violet | White

Black +
Lavender Lace (1:1)

15

*This pattern may be hand-traced or photocopied for personal use only.
It appears here at full size.*

Faux Finish

1 Basecoat the plate Dolphin Grey with the ¾-inch (19mm) oval wash brush.

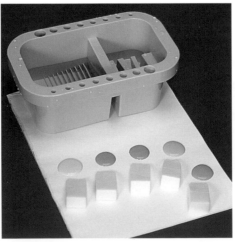

2 Place puddles of Ice Storm Violet, Lilac, Green Sea, Lavender Lace and Dolphin Grey on the palette. Have ready one clean stencil sponge to use for each color.

3 With the 1-inch (25mm) flat, dampen the surface of the plate with water.

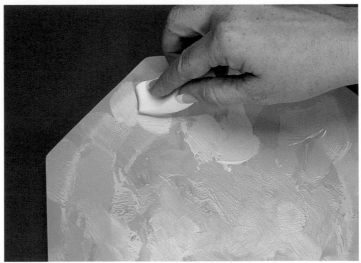

4 While the plate is still wet, load one of the sponges with Dolphin Grey. Make slip-slap Xs randomly on the plate. Leave some of the dry base coat exposed for other colors to be applied.

5 Pick up Lavender Lace on a clean sponge and add slip-slap Xs in some areas where you did not place Dolphin Grey.

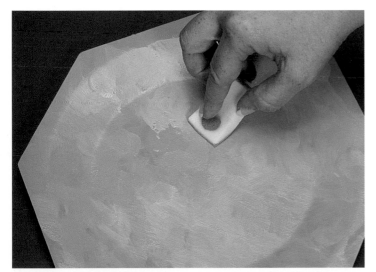

6 Without adding more paint, use the Dolphin Grey sponge to soften the edges, blending the Lavender Lace and Dolphin Grey edges where they meet. Do not overblend; you want the background to have a textured appearance.

7 Next load a clean stencil sponge with Green Sea and slip-slap Xs randomly on the plate.

Faux Finish, continued

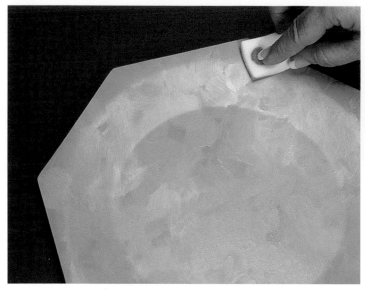

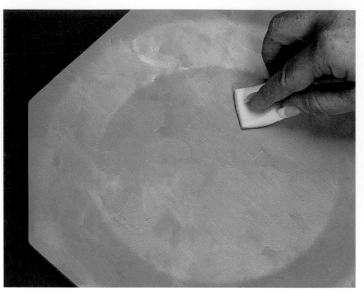

8 Again, soften the edges of the Green Sea with the Dolphin Grey sponge.

9 Load a clean sponge with Lilac and make slip-slap Xs on the plate. Soften the edges with the Dolphin Grey sponge.

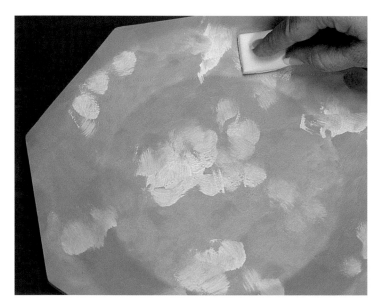

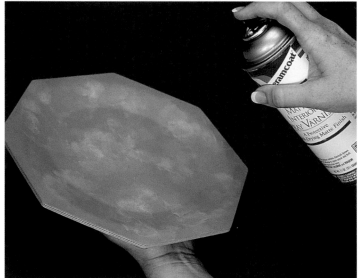

10 Load a clean sponge with Ice Storm Violet and slip-slap Xs randomly on the plate. Be sure to place some Ice Storm Violet in the area where the bird will be placed to give the appearance of a backlight. Soften the edges with the Dolphin Grey sponge.

11 Allow the paint to dry thoroughly, then apply two coats of matte spray varnish to the surface. This will protect the background so it won't be disturbed if you need to clean up a mistake when you're painting the bird.

Pattern

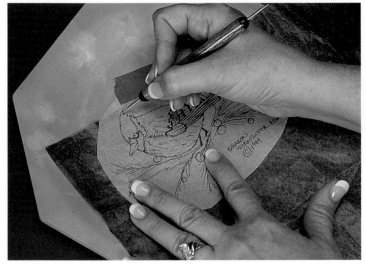

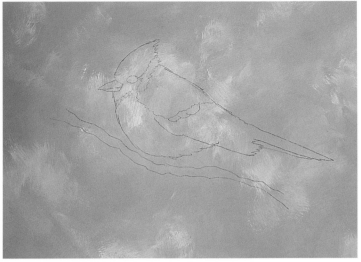

12 Trace the pattern onto tracing paper and attach it to the surface with low-tack tape. Slide gray graphite paper under the tracing paper and, using your stylus, transfer the basic outline of the bird to the plate. There's no need to apply the feather details until later.

13 Once the pattern is transferred, check the design on the plate and correct any shaky lines. The tail feathers, especially, should be very straight and sharp.

Base Coat for Bird

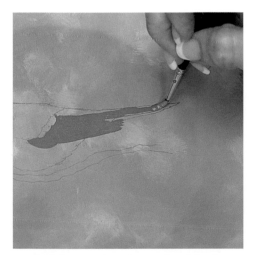

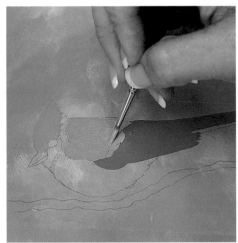

14 Basecoat the wing and tail feathers with the no. 3 round loaded with Ocean Reef Blue.

15 Clean this brush and use it to basecoat the head and back with Blue Jay.

16 Basecoat the light patches around the eyes and behind the neck with Periwinkle Blue using the no. 0 round.

Base Coat for Bird, continued

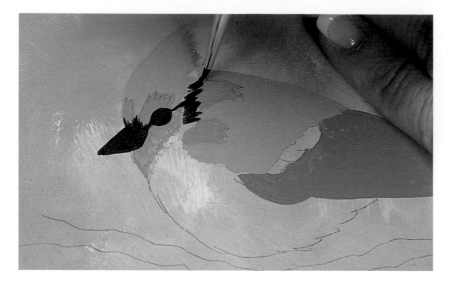

17 Basecoat the beak and eye with Black. Still using the no. 0 round brush, base in the neck feathers following the directional flow diagram. Paint these strokes sideways behind the eye, up and down behind the head and downward between the beak and the chest.

Feather Detail

18 After the base coat is dry, transfer the bird details of the pattern with the graphite paper and stylus. Be careful to keep all lines for tail feathers very straight.

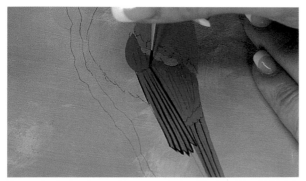

19 With the 18/0 liner, mix equal amounts of water and Black to an inky consistency. Load the brush as described on page 11, then outline the individual tail feathers.

Feathers Directional Flow

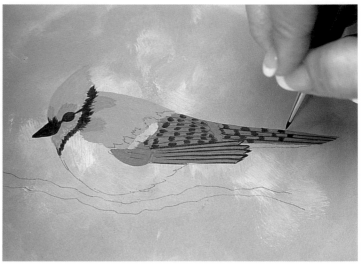

20 Clean the 18/0 liner and mix equal amounts of water and Blueberry to an inky consistency. Use this mix to outline the feathers on the wing.

21 Load the no. 0 round with inky Black and paint small lines to make the spot pattern on the wing and tail. The lines represent the individual feathers that make the spotted pattern.

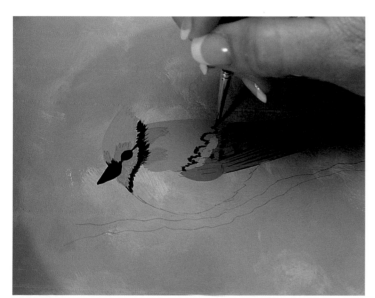

22 Tap small Black lines at the top of the wing, using the no. 0 round. These individual lines create the zigzag pattern above the wing.

23 Thin Lavender Lace with water to an inky consistency with the no. 0 round.

Feather Detail, continued

24 Blot your brush on a dry paper towel. Dip the brush in the thinned paint and pull it out a bit. Splay out the bristles in a half circle.

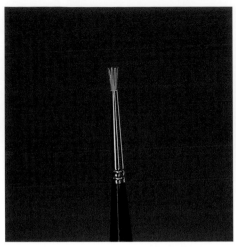

25 The bristles will now be separated and the strokes made with the brush will be feathery, like the many individual hairs of a rake brush. For this project you will be working in small areas, so this technique allows you to make a rake brush from a small brush.

26 Overstroke the areas that are Periwinkle Blue with the Lavender Lace. Each time you reload the brush, splay the bristles to achieve that feathery look.

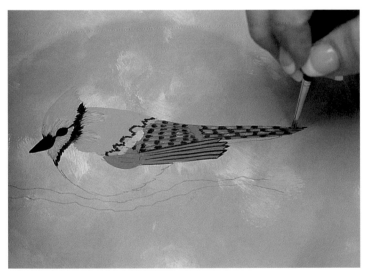

27 Using the same brush and technique, highlight the blue areas of the back and tail with a tiny touch of Lavender Lace.

28 Using the 18/0 liner, highlight the blue part of the bird's wing with the same mixture of inky Lavender Lace.

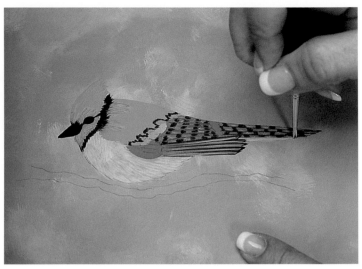

29 Thin Ice Storm Violet with water to an inky consistency. Load and fan out the no. 0 round brush as before. Pull small strokes to highlight the chest and coverts (the small feathers covering the bases of the quills of the wings and tail). Make short almost comma-like strokes for the feathers on the chest. You are only highlighting the chest with these strokes; do not cover the entire chest. The background of the plate will show through on the chest for dark color variations.

30 Continue with these little strokes along the bottom of the tail feathers.

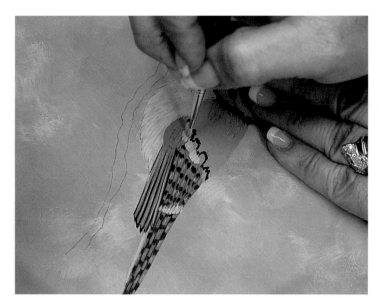

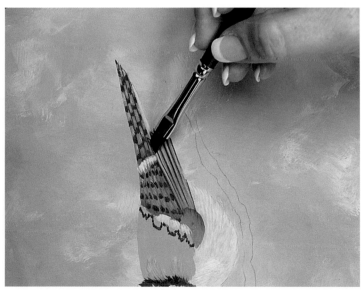

31 Paint highlight feathers on the small feathers below the zigzag line of black feathers.

32 Side load the long side of the ¼-inch (6mm) angle shader with Blueberry. Float color at the base of the tail and on the top and side of the wing to shade and separate feathers as needed. Also float along the outside edge of the small blue feathers in front.

Feather Detail, continued

33 With the same side-loaded brush on its side, zigzag short wiggly strokes on the back and head to create the appearance of depth and feathers. Do not cover all the previous color; you want to still see all the previous colors used.

34 Thin White with water to an inky consistency and load on the no. 0 round, splaying the bristles as described previously. Pull short highlight strokes at the top of the chest, on the coverts, the area below the tail and just a few light strokes in the Periwinkle Blue area around the eyes.

Eye

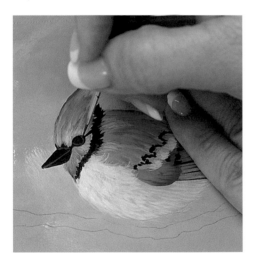

35 Using the 18/0 liner, mix Black and Lavender Lace to create a gray. Thin this gray with water to an inky consistency. Load the brush with this mixture, as described on page 11. With the brush handle straight up and down, apply a very narrow line on the beak and around the eye to create a rim.

36 Side load the ⅛-inch (3mm) angle shader with Ocean Reef Blue. Paint a very little C-stroke at the top of the eye.

37 With the tip of the 18/0 liner, pick up a tiny bit of White. Tap a little color in the upper front area of the eye for a sparkle.

Main Branch and Feet

38 With the no. 3 round loaded with Brown Velvet, base the branch with one long stroke. Load the 18/0 liner with Black and paint lines for the bird's feet.

Branches and Berries

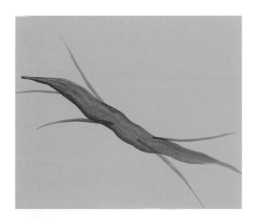

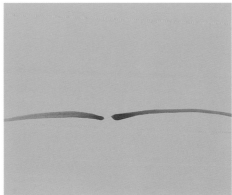

39 Use a no. 0 script liner to pull stems from the main branch with inky Brown Velvet. (For steps 39 through 44, the images at far left show the main branch, the images at left show the greenery along the outside of the plate.)

40 Create pine needles by stroking short lines with the no. 1 round brush loaded with inky Pine Green. Rinse the brush and overstroke using inky Green Sea.

41 Basecoat the berries with Opaque Red on the no. 1 round. Vary the berries in size, but keep them all round.

42 Side load the ⅛-inch (3mm) angle shader with Chocolate Cherry and float a C-stroke on one half of each berry—go all the way to the outside edge with the float. Allow to dry. Then highlight each berry opposite the shaded side with a flip-float of Lilac in a small patted sphere. Keep the loaded edge of the angle shader toward the center of the sphere highlight.

To create a flip-float, side load the brush, then apply the paint where you want the color to be the strongest. Flip the brush over, placing the loaded edge of the brush on the previously applied float, and apply the color again. The color ends up strongest in the center and fades out in all directions.

43 Load the no. 3 round with Ice Storm Violet and tap puddles of snow randomly on the branches and in-between the berries. Using the 18/0 liner, tap a tiny dot on each berry as a sparkle.

44 Load the liner brush with White and tap highlight puddles over the snow. Do not cover all of the Ice Storm Violet—use the White very sparingly.

45 Measure ½ inch (1.2cm) in from the edge of the plate. Paint a border around the plate with Chambray Blue. Load inky Opaque Red in the liner brush and pull a thin line between the border and the edge of the faux finish.

When dry, paint with two or three coats of brush-on matte varnish.

Cozy Red Cardinal

I have always loved the color complement of red and green. So when I decided to depict a bright red cardinal, it seemed a natural choice to paint him on a green background. This cardinal is surprisingly quick and easy to paint. My students fell in love with him because he painted up so quickly. They decided he was the perfect holiday gift!

I had so much fun painting this cardinal, I decided he also needed to go on a denim shirt so he could go everywhere with me! Instructions for painting the shirt begin on page 40.

MATERIALS

SURFACE

Small wood memory book from Walnut Hollow, supplied by Viking Woodcrafts, Inc. (Alternate surface: 9½"[24cm] octagonal plate from Viking Woodcrafts shown on page 28)

BRUSHES

Robert Simmons Expression

no. 1 script liner
no. 0 round
no. 1 round
no. 2 round
no. 6 round
⅛" (3mm) angle shader
⅜"(10mm) angle shader
½" (12mm) angle shader
no. 8 flat
¾" (19mm) flat

Robert Simmons AquaTip

½" (12mm) oval wash
¾" (19mm) oval wash
¼" (6mm) oval mop

Loew-Cornell

18/0 short liner

ADDITIONAL SUPPLIES

Delta Gel Blending Medium
Delta Matte Interior Spray Varnish
ruler
drinking glass or circle template
soapstone or white chalk pencil
white graphite paper
gold leaf adhesive
gold leafing
Delta Gel Stain Medium
Delta Matte Interior Varnish

DELTA CERAMCOAT ACRYLICS

White	Light Foliage Green	Seminole Green	Pine Green
Oasis Green	Alpine Green	Dark Foliage Green	Black Green
Spice Brown	Chocolate Cherry	Hippo Grey	Black
Opaque Yellow	Antique Gold	Tangerine	Opaque Red
Chocolate Cherry + Opaque Red (1:1)			

This pattern may be hand-traced or photocopied for personal use only. It appears here at full size.

Note that the directional flow lines for the feathers are on this pattern. If you wish, you may transfer these lines for guidance while you're painting. Or you may simply refer back to this image when you're painting the feathers.

Faux Finish

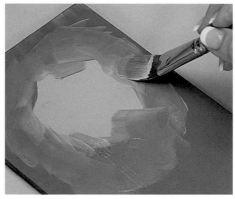

1 Take the memory book apart, removing all brackets and screws. Sand and seal each piece, then sand each piece again. Basecoat the front and back pieces with Alpine Green using the ¾-inch (19mm) oval wash.

Load the ½-inch (12mm) oval wash with blending gel, then load with Oasis Green. Apply the color on the upper center of the surface so it will be behind the cardinal when the pattern is transferred. (For the cardinal plate, place Oasis Green in the center of the plate and blend into darker colors toward the outside edges of the plate.)

2 Pinch out any excess paint from the brush on a dry paper towel. Reload the brush with blending gel, then load the brush with Alpine Green. Paint this color around the Oasis Green. If at any time the paint begins to drag, add more blending gel. Pinch out the brush with a paper towel, then blend the two colors until you do not see a hard line between the colors.

3 Add Dark Foliage Green and blending gel toward the bottom of the surface and a little in the upper corners. (For the cardinal plate, extend Dark Foliage Green all the way around the Alpine Green.)

4 Pinch out the brush with a paper towel and blend the Dark Foliage Green into the still-wet Alpine Green, as with previous colors.

5 Add Black Green with blending gel to the very bottom portion of the surface, around the Dark Foliage Green.

6 Pinch out the brush with a paper towel and blend into the still-wet Dark Foliage Green. Remember to add more blending gel as needed for a nice gradation of color. Let dry completely, or force dry with a hair dryer and allow the piece to cool entirely. Spray with two or three coats of matte spray to protect the background.

Pattern

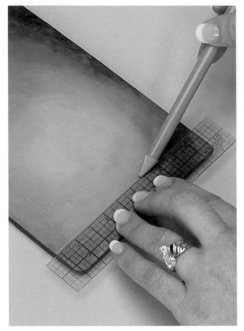

7 With a ruler and a soapstone (or white chalk pencil), make a line ¾ inch (1.9cm) in from the edge on the top and bottom of the front piece. (Make the line ½ inch [1.2cm] from the edge if painting on the plate.)

8 Use a circle template or a drinking glass to make a curve for the end of the line nearest the book binding. See finished piece on page 39 for guidance on placement.

9 Transfer the basic outline of the bird, including the face and tips of individual feathers, with white graphite paper and a stylus.

Base Coat for Bird

10 With the no. 6 round brush, basecoat the feathers with Opaque Red. Make short stokes, pulling from the beak area of the bird and lifting at the end of each stroke to create the look of feathers. Follow the contours of the bird. Some of the background color will show through—this will serve as some of the shading on the bird.

11 Basecoat the beak with the no. 2 round brush loaded with Tangerine. You may need to use two or three coats to completely cover the background.

Clean the brush and load it with Black, then basecoat the feathers around the beak and in eye area. Follow the directional flow lines on page 30 as you pull these strokes.

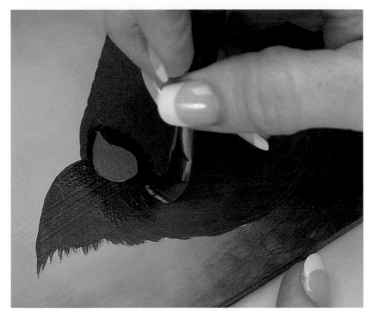

12 Double load the no. 8 flat brush with Opaque Red and Black (see page 116 for instructions on double loading). Place the Black side of the brush on the black part of the cardinal's face and the red half of the brush on the red part of the face. Wiggle the brush back and forth between these sections to soften the edge between the base coat colors and to create the appearance of feathers.

13 Transfer the details of the feathers to the surface with white graphite paper and a stylus.

Shading on Feathers

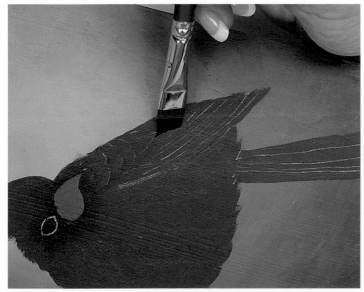

14 Side load a ⅜-inch (10mm) angle shader with Chocolate Cherry. Shade under each shoulder feather with the angle of the brush.

15 Continue with the Chocolate Cherry and shade under the wing and across the base of the tail.

Shading, continued

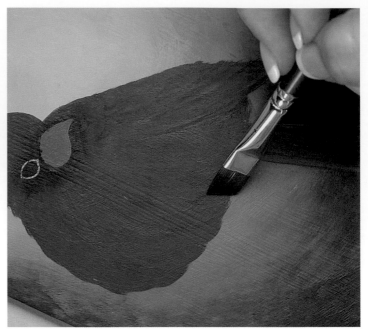

16 Shade the long wing and tail feathers with Chocolate Cherry, using the chisel edge of the brush to create both the shading and a sharp definition between the feathers. Let dry, then erase the pattern lines on the wing.

17 Continuing with the ⅜-inch (10mm) angle shader side loaded with Chocolate Cherry, add a little shading on the chest of the cardinal. Wiggle the brush back and forth while applying pressure to make these chest feathers.

18 Side load the ⅜-inch (10mm) angle shader with Opaque Red and start building the highlights. Float the color on top of each shoulder feather.

19 Then float the Opaque Red down each long feather on the tail and wing, angling the brush again for a thin highlight.

20 Continue with Opaque Red and lighten the chest with up-and-down zigzag lines. Do the same on the head.

21 Side load the same brush with a small amount of Tangerine. Reinforce the Opaque Red highlights with Tangerine, but do not completely cover the Opaque Red.

22 Continue with the Tangerine, reinforcing the Opaque Red highlights on the tail, chest and head.

Detail on Feathers

23 Side load the ⅜-inch (10mm) angle shader with Chocolate Cherry. With the edge of the brush, detail the shoulder feathers with short lines that follow the contours of the feathers. On the tail feathers paint small diagonal lines.

Beak

24 Trace the line for the beak and the stems of the greenery onto the surface with white graphite paper and a stylus.

25 Side load the ⅛-inch (3mm) angle shader with Opaque Red. Shade the bottom of the beak and along the top of the beak line.

26 Side load the ⅛-inch (3mm) angle shader with Opaque Yellow. Pat a small flip-float on the top section of the beak, and float the yellow along the top edge of the bottom of the beak. (See page 26 for an explanation of a flip-float.)

Eye

27 Side load the ⅛-inch (3mm) angle shader with Spice Brown and paint a small C-stroke in the eye. Load the 18/0 liner with thinned Hippo Grey and outline the eye. Use the same brush to add a White sparkle in the eye. Thin Black and load the 18/0 liner to paint the line in the beak.

Branches

28 Load the ½-inch (12mm) angle shader with straight Spice Brown, and basecoat the branches of the tree using the chisel edge of the brush. The main branches should be thicker than the offshoots.

29 Side load the same brush with Chocolate Cherry and shade the branches.

Greenery

30 Load the no. 1 round brush with Pine Green. Pull short strokes from the branches outward, creating needles. Turn the surface upside down or sideways so you always pull the needles toward yourself. Fill the branches with needles, but be sure to allow some of the brown branches to show through. If your brush dries out and the strokes start to skip in coverage, add a bit of water.

31 Clean the brush and load with Seminole Green. Again, pull strokes from the branches, adding fewer this time so that you can still see plenty of the dark pine strokes.

32 Clean the no. 1 round brush and load with Light Foliage Green. Add even fewer of these needles as they are just highlights.

Pinecones

33 With the soapstone, draw in ovals for the pinecones, placing them here and there on the branches. Do not put so many as to distract from the cardinal. Refer to the finished picture on page 39 for guidance on placement.

34 Load the no. 0 round with Spice Brown and paint small strokes on the side and front of the pinecone. Leave slight spaces in between the strokes.

35 Side load the ⅛-inch (3mm) angle shader with Chocolate Cherry and shade under each stroke.

36 Load the 18/0 liner with Antique Gold and tap a V at the end of each Spice Brown stroke. If needed, fill in any large empty spaces with small comma strokes of Antique Gold.

Gold Leafing

37 The cardinal and greenery are now complete. Make any final adjustments before starting with the gold leafing.

38 Basecoat the trim edges and small side piece of the memory book with Chocolate Cherry using the ¾-inch (19mm) flat brush. When dry, apply one coat of matte brush-on varnish over the Chocolate Cherry areas using the same brush. Let dry.

With the ½-inch (12mm) oval wash brush, or an old worn brush, evenly apply the gold leaf adhesive over the varnished Chocolate Cherry edges. The adhesive should be applied fairly thinly. Make sure the adhesive does not get on any of the green areas. Allow the adhesive to set until "clear" in appearance, about 20 minutes.

39 Wash your hands, then tear the gold leaf into little pieces. For variety, allow the leafing to wrinkle and create cracks and crevices. Pounce the gold leaf down onto the adhesive using your finger or a soft brush, such as the ¼-inch (6mm) oval mop.

40 Gently brush away the excess leafing with the soft brush, such as the ¼-inch (6mm) oval mop. If you find an empty tacky spot, put a small piece of leafing over it. In an empty area that is not tacky, repeat the adhesive step if the area is large or leave it as is if the area is small.

41 With a soft cloth, or with the rouging paper that comes with the gold leaf, gently rub the gold leaf to smooth it out and remove additional excess leafing.

42 Varnish the entire piece with a coat of matte spray varnish and let dry. Mix gel stain medium and Chocolate Cherry (2:1), then antique the gold leaf by applying a thin layer of the mix with the ¾-inch (19mm) flat.

43 Quickly buff off any excess stain with a clean paper towel or soft cloth. Allow to dry, or force dry with a hair dryer and allow to cool.

44 Apply a coat of brush-on varnish and let dry. Load the no. 1 script liner with a mix of Chocolate Cherry and Opaque Red (1:1) and a touch of water, if needed, to make the paint flow. Paint a line where the background and gold leafing meet at the top and bottom. (For the plate, load the brush with thinned Opaque Red only and apply thin linework all the way around the plate.)

45 Apply two or three coats of brush-on matte varnish to the pieces of the book. When dry, reassemble the book.

Cardinal on Fabric

MATERIALS
(continued)

SURFACE
Denim Shirt

PAINTS
Delta Fabric Dye
Brush-On Fabric Color
Red
Orange
Black
Red Light
Golden Yellow
Lemon Yellow
White
Light Brown
Light Green
Pigskin

Delta Starlite
Shimmering Fabric Color
Shimmering Hunter Green

BRUSHES
Robert Simmons Fabric Master
no. 1 liner
no. 4 round
¼" (6mm) angle scrubber
⅜"(10mm) angle scrubber

ADDITIONAL SUPPLIES
Delta Fabric Gel Medium
stiff board for mounting fabric shirt

1 Place a stiff board under the fabric. Pull the fabric tightly over the board, taping it down to secure the shirt to the board. Transfer pattern to the shirt with a transfer pen or lightly with graphite paper and a stylus.

Fabric Gel Medium helps the paint penetrate the fibers, so use it with all the fabric paints. Fully load a ¼-inch (6mm) angle scrubber with Fabric Gel Medium, then load with Red. Basecoat the bird, using the chisel edge of the brush and following the directional flow of the feathers. Pull the strokes from the inside of the bird to the outside. If the strokes start to drag, add more Fabric Gel Medium, and continue to paint the body, wing and tail areas.

Basecoat the beak with Orange on a no. 4 round fabric brush (a few coats are needed if painting on a blue surface). Basecoat around the beak with Black.

2 Let the base coat dry, then transfer the details for the wing, tail and eye with white graphite paper and a stylus. Be sure the fabric is pulled very tight and that you are working on a hard surface. Shade the bird with a mix of Red and Black (2:1), side loaded on the ¼-inch (6mm) angle scrubber. Jiggle the brush back and forth with pressure to apply the paint. Shade here and there on the chest and under the wing. Use the chisel edge of the brush to shade the lines for the individual feathers on the wing and tail. Highlight with Red Light, placing the highlights opposite the shading.

Shade the beak, especially where it attaches to the face, with a side load of Red. With Golden Yellow loaded on the tip of the no. 4 round brush, tap in a highlight on the top of the beak and paint in a narrow line on the bottom of the beak. Tap just a tiny bit of Lemon Yellow inside the top highlight.

3 Load the no. 1 liner with Black that has been thinned with water. Paint in the line on the beak. Mix a medium gray with Black and White for the rim inside the eye. Place a tiny dot of White on the upper right of the eye.

Load the ⅜-inch (10mm) angle scrubber with Light Brown and Fabric Gel Medium, and paint in the branches for the greenery using the chisel edge of the brush (see bare branch on the left side of the image).

Mix water and Shimmering Hunter Green to a consistency slightly thicker than ink. Heavily load the liner with paint, and pull strokes for the pine needles. Load the liner with Light Green (or Light Green plus White, if necessary for the color to show) and overstroke some of the previous needles. Mix a slightly lighter green by adding White, and paint just a few highlight strokes.

4 Load the tip of the round brush with Fabric Gel Medium, then add Light Brown to the brush. Tap in the base coat for pinecones (see page 37) and allow to dry completely. Load the ¼-inch (6mm) angle scrubber with Black and shade the pinecones with the chisel edge of the brush. Tap in highlights with Pigskin, using the liner brush.

Let the paint dry. Heat set the paint by placing the shirt in the dryer or by ironing the backside of the painting with a warm iron.

Least Chipmunk

My first up-close-and-personal encounter with a chipmunk was very educational. As a teenager, I was camping in an area where the chipmunks had become very tame and were used to people feeding them. As one climbed up on my lap to get the food out of my hand, I thought it would be fun to keep my hand closed to see his little tiny fingers try to open mine. After several failed attempts, he went to Plan B to open my fingers—his teeth, and I must say it worked very well! I let him open my hand with his fingers from then on!

This adorable little guy is a simple painting on the basswood round or the round box, or he would look wonderful on any small surface.

MATERIALS

SURFACE

5" (13cm) wooden bowl with cover from Viking Woodcrafts, Inc. (Alternate surface: 5" [13cm] basswood round from Walnut Hollow, supplied by Viking, shown on pages 42 and 51)

BRUSHES

Robert Simmons Expression
no. 10/0 liner
no. 0 round
no. 2/0 round
⅛" (3mm) angle shader
½" (12mm) wash
no. 12 flat
¾" (19mm) flat

Loew-Cornell
18/0 short liner

ADDITIONAL SUPPLIES

Delta Gel Stain Medium
Delta Crackle Medium
Delta Matte Interior Spray Varnish
Delta Matte Interior Varnish

DELTA CERAMCOAT ACRYLICS

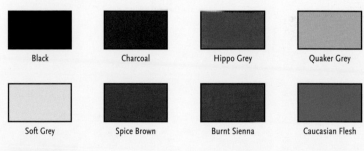

Black   Charcoal   Hippo Grey   Quaker Grey

Soft Grey   Spice Brown   Burnt Sienna   Caucasian Flesh

Spice Tan

Fur Directional Flow

Faux Finish

1 Sand the surface and seal with wood sealer. Then sand the surface again. Mix gel stain medium and Spice Brown (2:1), and with the ¾-inch (19mm) flat, apply stain to the entire surface, including the inside of the box. Allow to dry thoroughly, or heat set with a hair dryer. Protect the background with one or two coats of matte spray.

Paint the areas to be crackled with Black using the ¾-inch (19mm) flat brush. When dry, apply a fairly thin layer of crackle medium and let set for approximately 15 minutes (if using a different brand of crackle medium, follow the instructions on the bottle). With the no. 12 flat, apply a thin coat of Soft Grey using slip-slap Xs. The thinner the coat of paint, the smaller the cracks will be. Allow to dry at least overnight. (See project four, steps 3 through 5, for more detailed instructions on crackling.)

Transfer the chipmunk pattern onto the surface with graphite paper and a stylus.

Base Coat for Chipmunk

2 With the no. 0 round and Spice Brown (mixed with a touch of water, if needed, to make the paint flow smoothly), base in the dark areas of fur on the head and down the back. Use short strokes to begin creating the appearance of fur, and pull the strokes following the directional flow diagram, shown on page 44.

3 Base the "white" areas of the chipmunk with Quaker Grey, again using the no. 0 round and making the short fur-like strokes.

4 Clean the no. 0 round and load with Caucasian Flesh. Stroke fur into the Spice Brown areas around his arm and upper haunches.

5 With the no. 2/0 round, basecoat the eye with Black.

Tail

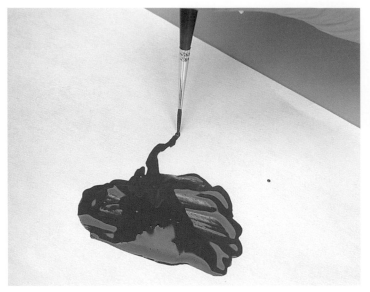

6 Thin Spice Brown with water (1:1) to an inky consistency, and load the no. 10/0 liner. Twist the handle of the brush as you pull the bristles out of the paint in order to get a fine tip.

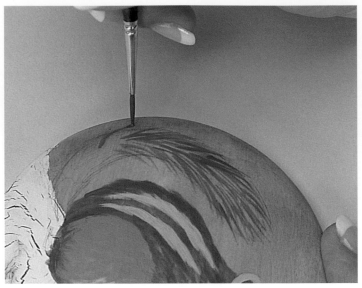

7 Pull long strokes of Spice Brown on the tail. Paint these strokes on all parts of the tail, but do not completely fill in the tail.

8 Load the no. 10/0 liner with inky Caucasian Flesh using the same technique as in step 6. Add strokes of this color to the fur on the tail. Clean the brush and repeat this step using inky Hippo Grey.

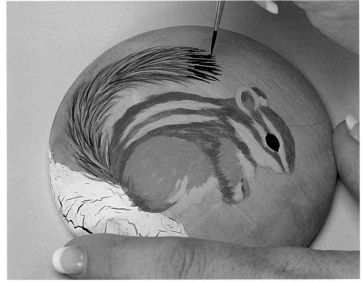

9 Load the no. 10/0 liner as described in step 6 with inky Black. Add some strokes to the main part of the tail. Then add a lot of strokes at the end of the tail for a very black tip. A black tip on the tail is one of the markings of the Least chipmunk.

Fur

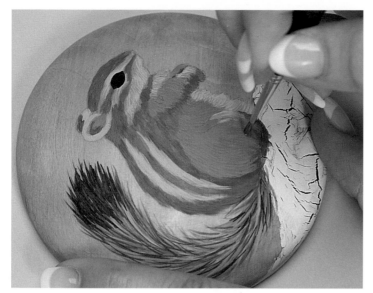

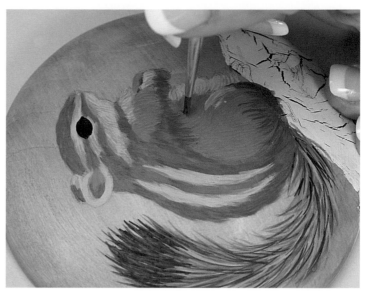

10 Load the no. 0 round with inky Hippo Grey. Applying pressure to the brush, fan the bristles as described on page 12, to give the round brush the appearance of a rake brush. Keeping the brush handle straight up and down, make short fur strokes all over the chipmunk. The heaviest concentration of Hippo Grey should be made in the areas basecoated with brown. Refer to the directional flow diagram often now and whenever you're painting fur.

11 Load the no. 0 round with inky Spice Brown and pull short strokes from the brown areas into the Caucasian Flesh area, using the same brush techniques described in step 10. Continue to use these techniques whenever you're painting the body fur in this project. Wherever two basecoat colors are touching, weave bits of fur into the neighboring color to soften the hard edge where the different colors meet and to add the appearance of fur density.

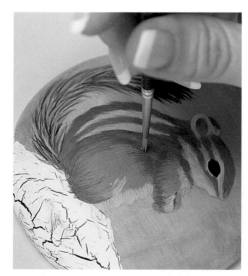

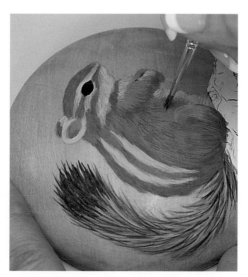

12 Load the no. 0 round with inky Caucasian Flesh and, starting in the Caucasian Flesh area, pull strokes into the Spice Brown area.

13 Load the no. 0 round with inky Burnt Sienna and add strokes of fur into the Caucasian Flesh areas.

14 Thin Spice Tan with an equal amount of water and load the no. 0 round brush as described in step 10. With this color add highlights to the center of the Caucasian Flesh area.

Foot

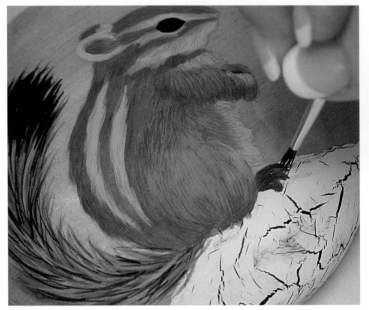

15 Basecoat the fur on the foot with Spice Brown using the no. 0 round. Using the same brush, shade the foot with short fur strokes of inky Charcoal.

16 Highlight the feet with inky Spice Tan. Load the 18/0 short liner brush with inky Black, and add the delicate claws.

Fur Details

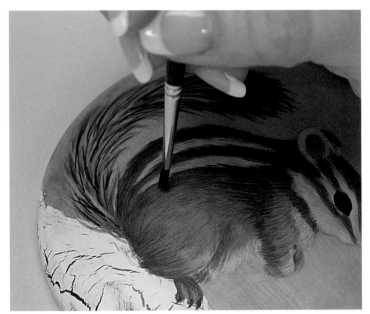

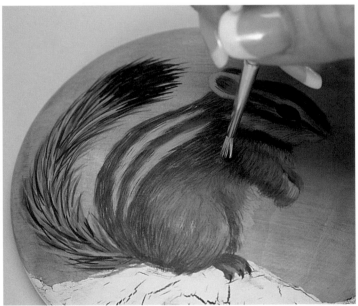

17 Load the no. 0 round with inky Charcoal and add a few strokes of fur to darken the brown areas.

18 Load the no. 0 round with inky Soft Grey and add a few strokes of fur in the dark areas for highlights.

19 Add inky Soft Grey to highlight the light areas down the back, on the belly and on the face.

20 Load the no. 10/0 liner with inky Spice Tan, using the same technique as in step 6, and add a few longish strokes in the tail. Do the same with Charcoal, then Burnt Sienna and then Soft Grey, each thinned to an inky consistency.

Eye

21 For the eye, make a C-stroke with Spice Brown using the ⅛-inch (3mm) angle shader side loaded on the long end of the hairs of the brush.

22 Load the 18/0 liner with inky Hippo Grey and outline the eye. Load the brush with straight Soft Grey and add a tiny dot sparkle in the upper-right corner of the eye. Then put a tiny comma stroke in the lower left side of the pupil for a highlight.

Whiskers

23 Load the 18/0 liner with inky Charcoal, and pull thin lines out from the bottom of the face (the muzzle) for the whiskers.

Faux Finish

24 Mix gel stain medium and Spice Brown (2:1). With the ½-inch (12mm) wash brush, slip-slap Xs of color on the crackled part of the lid, leaving some pure Soft Grey areas showing. Use the ¾-inch (19mm) flat to apply the Spice Brown stain mix to the bottom of the box. Soften any hard edges with a soft towel.

25 Mix gel stain medium with Charcoal (2:1) and, with the ½-inch (12mm) wash, slip-slap Xs over the crackled areas of the lid. Be sure to add some Charcoal stain under the chipmunk to set him on the rock. Use the ¾-inch (19mm) flat to apply the Charcoal stain to the bottom part of the box.

26 Allow all paint to dry thoroughly, then apply several thin coats of brush-on matte varnish for protection.

This project could be painted on any small surface, including a small basswood round, as shown below.

Tree Squirrel

I have always loved watching squirrels at play, whether they are up in the mountains or bouncing around in a park. They bring back fond memories of our family vacations in northern Colorado—I could watch them for hours! Alert to every movement around them, they can jump up any tree. They are continually hunting for food and safety. And their tiny fingers are amazingly adept at opening all those seeds and nuts, which are staple items in their diet.

When painting this cute little guy, your fur strokes should be long and graceful on his big fluffy, animated tail, which is the most recognizable part of the squirrel. The fur gradually gets shorter and shorter moving up the body until the hairs are no bigger than tiny dots on the head and face.

MATERIALS

SURFACE
7" (18cm) basswood round from Walnut Hollow, supplied by Viking Woodcrafts, Inc.

BRUSHES
Robert Simmons Expression
no. 0 round
no. 2 round
no. 4 round
⅛" (3mm) angle shader
½" (12mm) flat
¾" (19mm) flat

Loew-Cornell
18/0 short liner
¼" (6mm) filbert rake

ADDITIONAL SUPPLIES
2" (51mm) foam brush
Delta Gel Stain Medium
Delta Crackle Medium
Delta Matte Interior Spray Varnish
soapstone or white chalk pencil
Delta Matte Interior Varnish

DELTA CERAMCOAT ACRYLICS

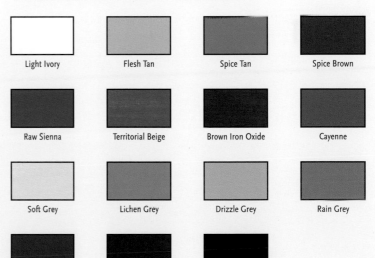

Light Ivory	Flesh Tan	Spice Tan	Spice Brown
Raw Sienna	Territorial Beige	Brown Iron Oxide	Cayenne
Soft Grey	Lichen Grey	Drizzle Grey	Rain Grey
Storm Grey	Charcoal	Black	

Background and Tree

1 Mix gel stain medium plus Spice Brown (2:1) with a palette knife until thoroughly blended.

2 Apply stain mix evenly to the surface with the 2-inch (51mm) foam brush, and allow to dry completely. Lightly spray surface with two or three coats of matte spray to protect the stain.

3 Transfer the tree pattern onto the surface. Basecoat the tree with Black using the ¾-inch (19mm) flat brush, painting the strokes in the direction you wish the cracks in the tree to run. Let dry completely.

Tree, continued

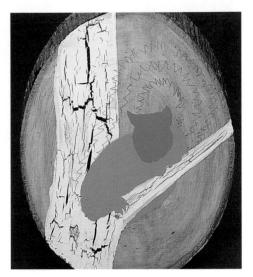

4 Apply the crackle medium with the ¾-inch (19mm) flat brush, taking care to keep the medium on the trunk. Make sure you have an even coverage so that it all sets up at the same rate. Allow medium to set for approximately 20 minutes, but read the directions on the bottle to verify how long to dry crackle medium before applying your top coat of paint. Wash your brush thoroughly with brush cleaner and rinse.

5 Apply a coat of Soft Grey with the same brush, painting over the partially dry crackle medium. Pull your stroke in the direction you want the cracks to run. Allow paint and crackle to dry completely, about 24 hours.

6 Using your stylus, transfer the squirrel pattern to the surface with dark graphite paper. Basecoat the head and ears with Territorial Beige using the no. 4 round brush. Basecoat the body, hands and feet with Rain Grey. You may need to apply two coats to cover where the squirrel is in front of the tree.

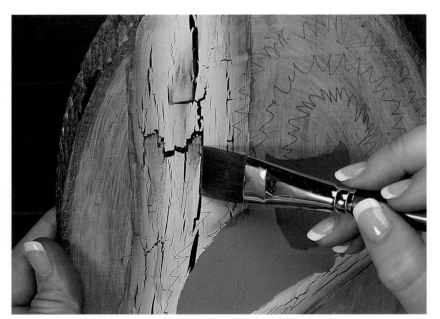

7 Side load the ¾-inch (19mm) flat with Storm Grey. Place the loaded edge of the brush on the edge of the tree and shade all the outer edges of the tree.

8 Use the same brush to float along some of the cracks of the tree trunk. Do this randomly, to create the appearance of natural bark. Shade under the squirrel, to set him down on the branch.

Tree, continued

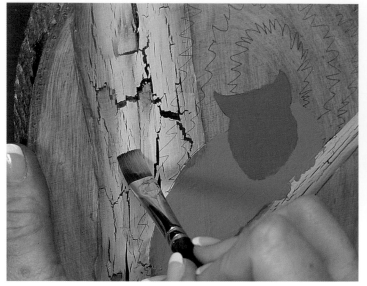

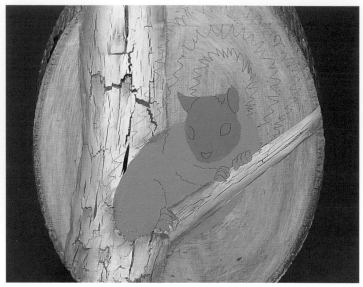

9 Side load the ½-inch (12mm) flat brush with Lichen Grey and float some light areas on the tree. Leave some of the Soft Grey showing through.

10 Transfer the pattern details onto the surface with graphite paper and a stylus.

Fur Directional Flow

Fur on Tail

11 Load an inky mixture of water and Territorial Beige (1:1) onto the ¼-inch (6mm) filbert rake brush, as described on page 12. To paint the inner ring of the tail, first apply pressure, then lift the brush to get fine hairlike ends.

Clean the brush and load with thinned Storm Grey, for the second ring on the tail. Starting at the end of the Territorial Beige, pull strokes out, again lifting at the end of the stroke. After making a few strokes, turn the surface and pull strokes from the middle of the gray into the Territorial Beige to start weaving the colors.

12 Clean the brush and load with inky Rain Grey. Again, paint the strokes going out toward the edge. Then turn the surface and, with the same technique, pull strokes into the dark gray tail fur.

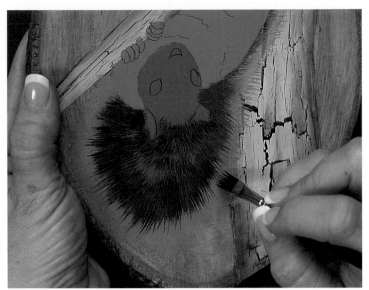

13 Darken the Territorial Beige area of the tail by stroking hairs of inky Storm Grey, using the same brush and technique. Add Charcoal strokes to darken and create a shaded appearance. Overstroke the Storm Grey ring of the tail with Charcoal, again pulling the strokes toward the outside, then to the inside.

14 Clean the brush and load with inky Drizzle Grey. Stroke this color on the outside for a light gray ring of fur, varying the strokes in length so that they look more natural.

15 Load the brush with Soft Grey and add a few light hairs, this time using the chisel edge of your brush. Add just a few of these strokes here and there. These strokes will be thicker than the previous hairs.

Fur on Body

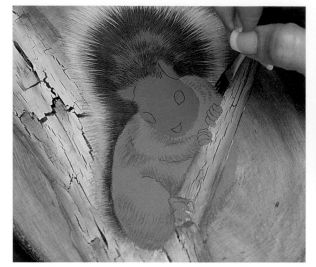

16 Load the ¼-inch (6mm) filbert rake with Storm Grey and begin to add darker fur strokes to the body. Be sure these strokes are much shorter than those on the tail.

17 Darken the shaded areas with short strokes of Charcoal. These strokes are all on top of the Storm Grey, but do not cover the Storm Grey strokes completely. There should be a transition of color from Rain Grey to Storm Grey to Charcoal.

Tip

The closer to the animal's nose, the shorter the fur. Therefore, the fur on an animal's tail and even its body will be longer than on its face.

18 Load the brush with Drizzle Grey and bounce short strokes into the light areas of the body. Then load the brush with Soft Grey and add this to the lightest areas, under the chin, on the belly and haunches, plus a little along the back. Again, leave some of the Drizzle Grey showing through to transition into the Rain Grey.

19 To incorporate the colors of the head on the body, add a little Territorial Beige and Raw Sienna to the Rain Grey areas of the body. Use the ¼-inch (6mm) filbert rake and the same technique described previously.

Fur on Face

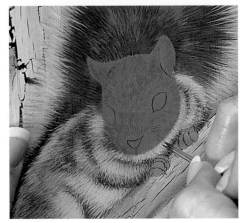

20 If some of the hairs you stroked onto the body happen to overlap onto the head, re-basecoat those areas with Territorial Beige. Load the no. 0 round brush with Storm Grey, as described on page 12, to create the effect of a rake brush. Keeping the brush handle straight up and down, bounce the tiny fur strokes on the head. Keep them very short. They will look very freckly at this point—don't worry and keep going!

21 Load the brush with Spice Tan. Paint tiny strokes around the eyes, on the ear tufts, randomly on the head and in small V-shape areas between each eye and the nose.

22 Load the brush with Rain Grey and tap in tiny dots of fur. Use just the tip of the brush hairs and bounce in the color.

23 Side load the ½-inch (12mm) flat with Storm Grey and, with the paint to the outside, float around the head to give the head dimension and to curve the edges into the background. Load the 18/0 short liner with inky Flesh Tan and tap in tiny strokes around the eyes and on the ears. Add just a few Flesh Tan dots randomly around the head with the tip of the brush.

24 Load the 18/0 liner with Charcoal and darken the darkest areas, tapping in tiny strokes of color. Clean the brush and load with Light Ivory. Tap this into the lightest areas of the face.

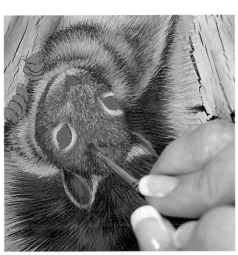

25 Load the no. 0 round with Cayenne and accent the tufts of the ears and between the right eye and nose.

Eyes and Nose

26 With the no. 2 round brush, basecoat the eyes with Black. Basecoat the nose with Cayenne. Sketch in the iris of the eye with a soapstone. Side load the ⅛-inch (3mm) angle shader with Raw Sienna and float a C-stroke in each eye with the loaded side of the brush down. Clean the brush and side load with Charcoal and float this around the nose.

27 Side load the ⅛-inch (3mm) angle shader with Light Ivory and float a tiny C-stroke highlight at the top of each eye. Side load again and tap a tiny puddle in the C-stroke to give a sparkle. If needed, redefine the edge of the eyes with Black using the 18/0 liner. Load the liner with inky Rain Grey and delicately create the rims at the corners of each eye.

Feet

28 Load the 18/0 liner with inky Storm Grey. Tap in tiny hairs to create the separation between each finger. Clean the brush and load with Soft Grey. Tap tiny hairs on the tops of the fingers for highlights.

29 Load the 18/0 liner with inky Charcoal and pull one thin, curved line at the end of each finger to create the claws.

Final Details

30 Side load the ¾-inch (19mm) flat with Brown Iron Oxide. Float a fairly wide shade around all the edges of the tree onto the stained background. Let dry completely.

31 Float the same color around the edge of the surface.

32 Color weave the fur as described on pages 72–74, until you are pleased with the results. Load the 18/0 liner with inky Charcoal and pull to create thin whiskers coming from the cheek. Sign and date your finished painting, then varnish with two or three coats of brush-on matte varnish.

Siberian Tiger

The Siberian tiger is a truly majestic creature. It is the largest of all the big cats, sometimes growing to be seven feet long and over six hundred pounds. This is one big kitty. Now I'm sure my "big kitty" at home thinks he could take on any other cat; after all he is about twenty pounds. But I fear that my darling Boxcar wouldn't stand a chance against this bigger brother!

The bold black stripes on orange and white make this an animal you cannot help but be in awe of. While painting this piece, take time with your color weaving to blend these beautiful colors into one another, but be careful not to lose the boldness of the black stripes.

Enjoy the beauty you have just created in this painting.

MATERIALS

SURFACE

11" x 14" (28cm x 36cm) multimedia board (or mat board) from Viking Woodcrafts, Inc.

BRUSHES

Robert Simmons Expression

no. 0 script liner
no. 2 round
no. 3 round
no. 6 chisel blender
no. 8 chisel blender
no. 8 flat
¼" (19mm) flat

Robert Simmons AquaTip

½" (12mm) oval mop
¾" (19mm) oval mop

Loew-Cornell

18/0 short liner
¼" (6mm) filbert rake

ADDITIONAL SUPPLIES

2" (51mm) foam brush
Delta Matte Interior Spray Varnish
gray chalk pencil
Delta Matte Interior Varnish

DELTA CERAMCOAT ACRYLICS

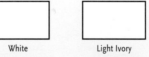
White | Light Ivory | Mudstone | Sandstone

Flesh Tan | Antique Gold | Dark Goldenrod | Caucasian Flesh

Burnt Sienna | Burnt Umber | Chocolate Cherry | Blue Storm

Black

This pattern may be hand-traced or photocopied for personal use only. Enlarge at 125 percent to bring it up to full size.

Background

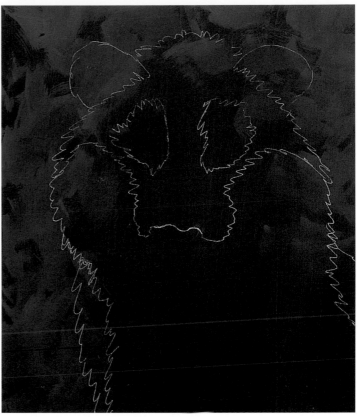

1 Basecoat the multimedia board with Black using the 2-inch (51mm) foam brush. Let dry. With Black still in the brush, load one corner of the foam brush with Blue Storm and lightly blend the blue and black on your palette. With a slip-slap motion, make loose Xs across the top and along the right and left side of the board with the blended corner. Let dry, then seal with matte spray to protect the faux finish.

2 Transfer the color breaks of the pattern onto the surface with white graphite paper and a stylus.

Fur Directional Flow

Base Coat

3 Using the ½-inch (12mm) oval mop brush, base all of the orange fur areas (refer to the picture at left) with Dark Goldenrod. Follow the directional flow diagram to apply each brushstroke, and lift the brush at the end of each stroke to begin to give the appearance of fur. Clean the brush and load with Mudstone, the base coat for the white fur areas. Base in the Mudstone. Again, follow the directional flow diagram and be sure to lift the brush at the end of each stroke. At this stage, the base coats will not appear smooth; this is desired to start giving a textured effect.

4 Side load the ¾-inch (19mm) oval mop brush with Black. Apply a flip-float in each ear, with the paint side of the brush toward the center of the ear. The color should gradually fade out leaving the edges Mudstone.

5 Transfer the pattern detail onto the surface with black graphite paper and a stylus.

Black Fur

6 Using the no. 3 round brush, basecoat the eyes with Black. Load the ¼-inch (6mm) filbert rake brush (as described on page 12) with inky Black and basecoat the black stripes. For the areas around the eyes, hold the brush almost straight up and down and make short fur strokes with the chisel.

7 In the other areas of the tiger, use the full width of the brush to pull the black stripe fur strokes.

Orange Fur

8 Load the same brush with inky Burnt Sienna. Apply this in the Dark Golden-rod areas on the face. Make very short strokes on and around the nose. The areas with the heaviest coverage should be along the sides of the nose. The strokes for the individual hairs will be lighter and wispier than those used for basecoating the black stripe. Keep the directional flow diagram in front of you and refer to it often.

9 Now add the Burnt Sienna to the Dark Goldenrod stripes, making the strokes short and wispy. Turn the board as necessary so that you always pull the strokes toward yourself.

10 Load the ¼-inch (6mm) filbert rake with inky Chocolate Cherry to darken in the Dark Goldenrod areas over the Burnt Sienna.

Then using a side-loaded ¾-inch (19mm) flat, flip-float a shade in the darkest areas at the sides of the nose. With the side-loaded brush, paint a zigzag shade along the edges of the tiger and here and there on the orange stripes.

White Fur

11 Load the ¼-inch (6mm) filbert rake with inky Sandstone. Begin to build the light fur areas, letting some of the Mudstone base coat show through. Use short, bouncy strokes around the eyes and mouth, graduating to longer strokes on the body.

12 When painting the stripes with Sandstone, weave the light color into the black stripes. To do this, start in the middle of the light stripe and pull strokes lightly into the black stripe. Don't forget to continually refer to the directional flow diagram!

13 Turn the surface around. Start the stroke in the same place as the previous stroke and pull toward yourself, in the opposite direction from the first stroke.

14 Load the brush with inky Flesh Tan. Overstroke the Sandstone beginning in the middle of the white areas, taking care to let some of the Sandstone and Mudstone show through. Use the same light, wispy strokes and pull some of the strokes into the black stripes from the center of the light. Repeat as before, turning the painting around and pulling in the opposite direction.

15 Lighten the white fur further with inky Light Ivory loaded on the ¼-inch (6mm) filbert rake. Overstroke the previously applied Flesh Tan, taking care to leave some of the Flesh Tan and all of the previous colors showing.

16 Load the ¼-inch (6mm) filbert rake with Black and pull very short strokes down from the mouth.

Eyes

17 Place the pattern over the eyes to make sure the shape has not changed. For a friendly-looking tiger, make sure the eyes are open; a tiger with squinty eyes will look angry. Transfer the pattern for the iris and pupils onto the surface. With the no. 2 round, basecoat the iris with Antique Gold, adding more coats as necessary to get complete coverage. If the pupils become misshapen or if you get the irises too close to the edge, take time to adjust them now.

18 Side load the no. 8 chisel blender with Burnt Sienna. With the color side up against the eyelid, float the color across the entire eye. Let this dry.

19 Clean the brush and load with a small side load of Black—this float should be narrower than the previous one. Overstroke the Burnt Sienna.

20 Side load the no. 6 chisel blender with Light Ivory, and apply a flip-float C-stroke in the center of the iris.

21 Clean the brush and side load with White, and float a C-stroke of White just below the eyelid.

22 Load the corner of the no. 6 chisel blender with White and place a puddle of paint for a sparkle in the White C-stroke. Load the 18/0 liner brush with inky Mudstone and paint a thin line to create the lower rim of the eye.

Nose

23 With the no. 2 round brush loaded with Caucasian Flesh, basecoat the nose. Float a little Mudstone on top of the nose with the no. 6 chisel blender and pull a few hairs up onto the bridge of the nose. Draw in the nostril lines for the next step.

24 With a no. 8 chisel blender, float Black around the outside of the nose, curving in to fill in the nostrils.

25 Lightly side load the no. 6 chisel blender with Black and float a little color on the inside of the nose, keeping the color side of the brush to the outside.

Ears

26 Side load the ½-inch (12mm) oval mop with Sandstone and float color all along the outside edge of each ear. Side load the same brush with Dark Goldenrod and float color down the inside half of each ear, over the previous float.

27 Load the ¼-inch (6mm) filbert rake with inky Sandstone, and stroke in fur on the ears, making short hairs on the ear edges and long hairs for tufts in front of the ears. Clean the brush and repeat with Flesh Tan. Clean the brush and load with Light Ivory, adding only a few of these lightest hairs.

Highlight Fur

28 Load the ¼-inch (6mm) filbert rake with thinned Antique Gold. Apply this where any two colors come together, especially where the golden and white stripes meet. This color adds a nice bright highlight, but be careful not to overdo it. Also, apply a little bit in the golden areas for highlight.

Color Weaving

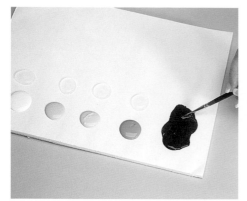

29 To give the fur depth and realism, you need to go back and add overlapping hairs in a number of different colors. Use the ¼-inch (6mm) filbert rake for all color weaving. Place puddles of Black, Dark Goldenrod, Flesh Tan, Sandstone and Light Ivory on your palette. Thin each with water (1:1), mixing with the side of the brush. Blot excess paint out of the brush.

30 Load the filbert rake with inky Black as directed on page 12. Starting with the brush in the middle of the black stripe, with very little pressure on the brush, tickle little hairs out into the neighboring stripes. Hold the brush straight up and down, and lift the brush at the end of the short stroke so the ends of the hairs do not get too heavy. All the fur should continue in the same direction as before—do not crisscross the hairs; the ends of the hairs should interweave.

31 Turn the surface and pull inky Black from the middle of the black stripe into its neighbor on the other side. Vary the lengths of the strokes, making some longer than others. Repeat for all the black stripes.

32 Next, clean the brush and load with inky Dark Goldenrod. Starting in the center of the orange stripes, pull hairs out into the neighboring stripes (in this case, black). Do not cover the Chocolate Cherry shading on the orange stripes.

33 Turn the surface and pull Dark Goldenrod from the center of the orange stripe, in the other direction. If your brush drags or the paint skips, add more water to the paint or reload the brush as needed.

34 In areas like this where the stripe changes from orange to white, be sure to carry a bit of the Dark Goldenrod into the white areas, so that there is not a hard edge between them.

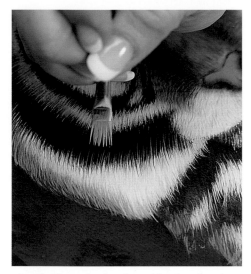

35 Clean the brush and load with inky Flesh Tan. Starting in the center of the white stripes, pull a few strokes out into the neighboring stripe.

36 Turn the surface and pull strokes into the neighboring stripe on the other side.

37 Load the brush with inky Sandstone and pull strokes over the Flesh Tan strokes. Paint fewer Sandstone hairs than Flesh Tan and keep the Sandstone toward the center of the light stripe.

38 Turn the surface and pull strokes of inky Sandstone from the light stripe into its neighbor on the other side.

39 Continue to pull strokes with Sandstone. Where the light stripe turns into orange, pull some light Sandstone strokes into the orange to soften the edge.

40 Load the brush with inky Light Ivory and pull strokes over the Sandstone. This is the lightest highlight, so add the least amount of this color. Again, highlights will be strongest in the center-most area of the light stripes. You want to see every color applied so far; this is what gives the fur so much depth.

Color Weaving, cont.   ## Shading on Tiger

41 Continue to color weave until you are happy with the way your tiger looks. This is a time-consuming process, but it really makes the animal fur look real. Apply a coat of matte spray, if desired, to protect your color weaving before proceeding to the next step.

42 With a side load of Burnt Umber on the ¾-inch (19mm) flat brush, place a float around the sides of the tiger's head, between the ears and down the back. The float around the edges of the tiger needs to follow the direction of the fur. Hold the brush on the chisel edge and make back-and-forth strokes (see image in step 43). This helps to set the tiger into the background. Make a flip-float on either side of the nose to make the sides recess a little.

43 Clean the brush and paint a soft float of Chocolate Cherry over the Burnt Umber from the previous step. Again, hold the brush on the chisel edge.

Freckles

44 With a gray chalk pencil, lightly draw three lines on the tiger's muzzle, following the contours of the mouth. With the 18/0 liner loaded with inky Black, place the freckles on these lines, using very short strokes to simulate fur. Vary the size of the freckles. If they get too dark, pull some Sandstone over them with the liner brush to lighten.

Whiskers

45 With a gray chalk pencil, draw in the whiskers, starting each at a different freckle and slightly arching out. Each time you paint this project, the whiskers will turn out different—that is fine because each tiger is different.

46 Using the no. 0 script liner, base a whisker with inky Sandstone. Hold the brush straight up and down, apply pressure at the freckle, then lift the brush gradually as you reach the tip of the whisker. Use your pencil lines as a guide, but do not worry if you miss the line as you are painting. The line for each whisker should be long and graceful, not forced.

47 Clean the brush and load with inky Black. Paint an even thinner line below each whisker. Keep a cotton swab handy to wipe off any mistakes, but do not worry if there is a little bit of space between the lines. Allow to dry, then erase the whisker guidelines.

48 Load the brush with inky White and lightly highlight the arc on some of the whiskers. Use the White also if you feel some of the whiskers are not showing up well enough.

Side load Black on the no. 8 flat brush and float a shadow around the nostrils, extending the shadow slightly beyond the nose. Sign and date the piece and allow it to dry thoroughly. Apply several coats of brush-on matte varnish to protect your painting.

Wild Cottontail Rabbit

At my parent's house in Nevada, there is a wonderful cottontail bunny that lives under the shed and only bounces out when it is safe. He loves to eat the goodies they leave out for him, but make no mistake, this is a wild rabbit, amazingly cute, and fast!

The rabbit's fur blends into the dry grasses in which he lives, serving to better protect him from predators. So in this painting, many of the colors used in the rabbit are repeated in the grass and background. This creates a subtle difference so that the wild cottontail rabbit looks at home.

The faux finish on the sides of the box is created with cotton balls and glazes of color (after all he is a cottontail rabbit!).

MATERIALS

SURFACE
9½" x 11" rectangular Bombay box (24cm x 28cm) with round ball feet by Valhalla Designs

BRUSHES
Robert Simmons Expression
no. 0 script liner
no. 2 round
no. 4 chisel blender
no. 6 filbert
no. 12 flat
¾" (19mm) flat
no. 1 flat basecoater
¾" (19mm) round basecoater

Robert Simmons Decorator Stencil
⅛" (3mm) stencil
¼" (6mm) stencil

Loew-Cornell
⅛" (3mm) filbert rake
¼" (6mm) filbert rake
18/0 short liner

ADDITIONAL SUPPLIES
Delta Gel Blending Medium
fuzz-free cotton balls
low-tack painter's tape
Delta Matte Interior Spray Varnish
Delta Matte Interior Varnish
wood glue

DELTA CERAMCOAT ACRYLICS

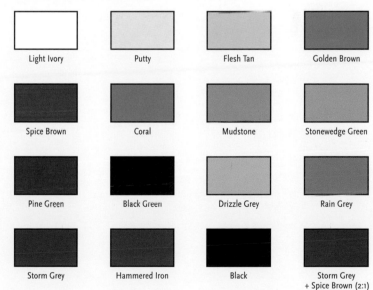

Light Ivory	Putty	Flesh Tan	Golden Brown
Spice Brown	Coral	Mudstone	Stonewedge Green
Pine Green	Black Green	Drizzle Grey	Rain Grey
Storm Grey	Hammered Iron	Black	Storm Grey + Spice Brown (2:1)

This pattern may be hand-traced or photocopied for personal use only. Enlarge at 139 percent to bring it up to full size.

Fur Directional Flow

Faux Finish

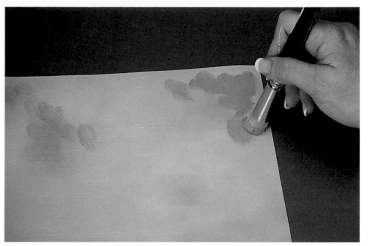

1 Sand the entire wood surface, and seal with wood sealer. Lightly sand again. Basecoat entire surface with Flesh Tan using the no. 1 flat basecoater—two coats may be needed for full coverage.

With the same brush, brush-mix blending gel with Flesh Tan and paint onto the lid of the box. You may leave the two lower corners exposed.

Apply Putty to a few areas in the upper center of the surface with the no. 1 flat basecoater. Pinch the bristles with a dry paper towel, then add a bit of Flesh Tan to the brush. Blend this on the palette, then use the brush to soften the edges where the Putty and Flesh Tan meet.

2 You will be blending and softening colors for the next three steps, so to keep the paint from drying too quickly, you may work on one section at a time. Or, if you like, dry thoroughly between colors so the blending gel does not get tacky. With the no. 1 flat basecoater, apply a thin coat of blending gel to the area in which you will be working. Pick up a little Stonewedge Green with the ¾-inch (19mm) round basecoater and pat in the color, mostly in the corners and where the ground will be. Without picking up more color on the no. 1 flat basecoater, soften the edges where the colors meet. Darken some areas by adding Mudstone to the surface with the dirty ¾-inch (19mm) round basecoater.

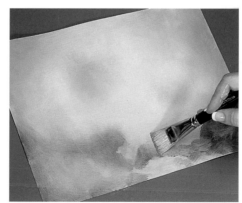

3 Soften the edges of the Mudstone using the dirty no. 1 flat basecoater and a light touch.

4 Let dry, or force dry with a hair dryer and allow to cool. Apply a thin layer of blending gel to the bottom part of the surface. Pat Hammered Iron on the ground area and slightly up the sides of the surface with the ¾-inch (19mm) round basecoater. Soften the edges with the dirty no. 1 flat basecoater.

5 Adjust the background colors until you are satisfied. Let dry. Spray with two or three coats of matte spray to protect the faux finish. Transfer the pattern onto the surface with black graphite paper and a stylus.

Base Coat for Fur

6 Load the ¼-inch (6mm) filbert rake with inky Golden Brown as described on page 12. Pull short fur strokes behind the head, down the back, behind the ears, around the eye and nose and on the legs, lifting the brush at the end of each stroke. Remember, the closer the fur is to the nose, the shorter it is. The body hairs will be a little longer.

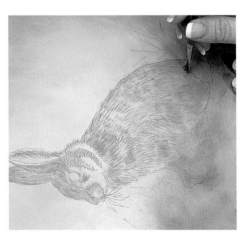

7 Load the ¼-inch (6mm) filbert rake with inky Rain Grey and paint short fur strokes on the rabbit's head, back and legs. Turn the surface as necessary so that you pull the strokes toward yourself.

8 Side load the no. 6 filbert with Coral and float it on the inside of the right ear.

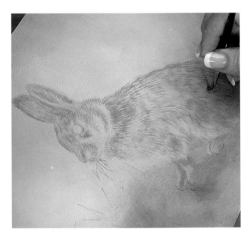

9 Load the ⅛-inch (3mm) filbert rake with inky Drizzle Grey and overstroke the Rain Grey and Golden Brown in the lightest areas. With the chisel edge of the brush, pull short fur strokes along the outside of the right ear. Remember to keep some of the background showing; it is the medium color of the rabbit.

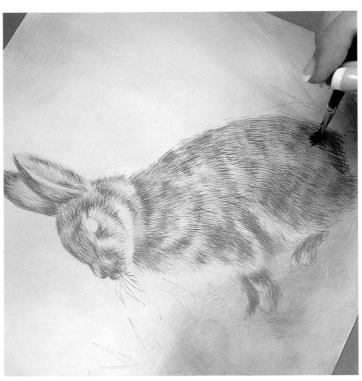

10 Load either the ⅛-inch (3mm) or ¼-inch (6mm) filbert rake, whichever you feel more comfortable using, with inky Spice Brown. Brush this over the Rain Grey and Golden Brown areas making sure the previous layers of color show through.

11 Using either (or both) of the filbert rakes, brush inky Storm Grey into the darkest fur areas.

12 With inky Light Ivory on either of the filbert rakes, brush fur strokes over the lightest areas. At this point, the fur is in, but you will still need to color weave it to get the appearance of soft, natural fur. You may color weave now, or if you're ready to take a break from fur, you may do it after the grass is complete. In this project, I did the color weaving after painting the grass. When you do color weave, rework all colors used as needed, remembering to use Flesh Tan as one of the fur colors.

Eye

13 Basecoat the eye with the no. 2 round loaded with Black. Side load the no. 4 chisel blender with Spice Brown. Float a C-stroke to create the iris within the Black base coat. Leave a narrow rim of black showing around the iris and a black area for the pupil. If your brown iris got too wide, go back with Black and reapply color in these areas.

14 With inky Rain Grey on the 18/0 liner, outline the bottom front and back of the eye to create the eye rim just inside the black. Load the brush with Light Ivory and add a sparkle dot in the upper right of the eye. In the lower left of the iris area, paint a small comma stroke for highlight.

Tail

15 Load your no. 6 filbert with Rain Grey and pat in the tail. Keep the strokes short, lifting at the ends, so the tail is light and fluffy.

16 Load the ¼-inch (6mm) stencil brush with Drizzle Grey. Pounce in the color on the tail to lighten it. Load the ⅛-inch (3mm) stencil brush with Flesh Tan and pounce in a small area to highlight.

Grass

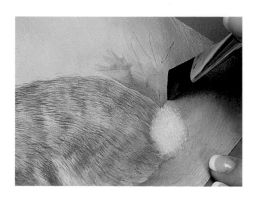

17 Side load the ¾-inch (19mm) flat with Storm Grey and scumble in dark areas at the corners of the surface and under and around the rabbit. Do not smooth out the strokes; keep this looking rough, since it will be grass. With what is left on the brush, add a bit of color to darken the upper corners, keeping the color side of the brush to the outside of the wood piece.

18 Side load the no. 12 flat with Storm Grey. To paint the individual grasses, jiggle the chisel edge of the brush back and forth to create the base of the grass.

19 Then pull the brush up to form the blade. Paint the Storm Grey grass in the area in front of the rabbit and a little below and behind the rabbit.

20 Side load the brush with Flesh Tan and paint in some lighter grass. Work back and forth with the Storm Grey and Flesh Tan until you achieve a loose suggestion of dried grass. This area is not neat and detailed because the rabbit is the focus of the painting.

21 Side load the brush with Stonewedge Green and add a few more blades of grass. Keep the grass looking messy. Place a few blades of Stonewedge Green grass in the rabbit's mouth.

22 Brush-mix Pine Green with water until fairly transparent. With the no. 12 flat, paint this wash over the grass in a loose slip-slap motion. Place a small float of Pine Green across the grass in the rabbit's mouth to create a light shadow (see grass in image for step 23).

23 With a transparent side load of Black Green on the same brush, fill in some of the spaces between the grasses and set the rabbit in the grass with a float of color.

Final Details

24 Mix a wash of water and a tiny dot of Coral. Side load this mix onto the ¾-inch (19mm) flat and slip-slap a transparent bit of color in all the corners of the surface and a little above the rabbit's back.

Whiskers

25 Color weave the fur, if you haven't already done so, until you are happy with the result. Remember to use all the colors of the fur, including Flesh Tan. When done, load the 18/0 liner with inky Rain Grey and delicately stroke in the whiskers.

Faux Finish on Sides of Box

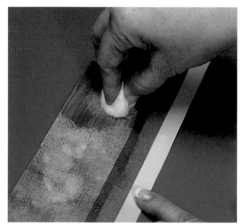

26 Place low-tack painter's tape about ½ inch (1.2cm) from the bottom of each side of the box. Rub the tape down firmly with an eraser. Create a mix of Storm Grey and Spice Brown (2:1). Then mix blending gel and the paint mix (2:1). Paint this mixture on one side of the box with the ¾-inch (19mm) round basecoater. Place a cotton ball on the surface, apply pressure and twist to remove some of the paint. Use varying amounts of pressure to get a mottled look. Repeat on all sides of the box, keeping the pattern as random as possible. Heat set with a hair dryer.

27 With the ¾-inch (19mm) flat, brush-mix a wash of mostly water and a tiny bit of Coral. Lightly slip-slap some of this mix over the finish you just created on each side of the box. Side load the brush with Storm Grey and float the color on the end of each side, to darken the corners.

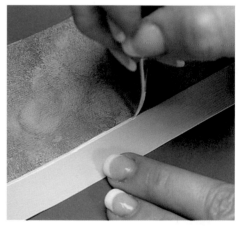

28 Carefully remove the tape. Load the no. 0 script liner with inky Light Ivory and paint a line to separate the faux finish from the Flesh Tan base coat on the sides as well as the lid of the box.

29 Paint the ball feet the same way you painted the sides of the box. Glue ball feet to the bottom four corners of the box.

30 To finish this project, varnish all surfaces with three or four coats of brush-on matte varnish.

Endangered Red Panda

This is a project inspired by one of my long-time students, Pat Neibert. She keeps me on my toes by popping up with interesting things she wants to paint; the red panda was one of them.

This adorable creature is fascinating! Residing in China, the red panda, an endangered animal, is much smaller than its more familiar cousin, the giant panda. Many zoos have these wonderful red pandas, so make sure to take a look.

Bamboo is their staple diet, so sitting in a tree munching on bamboo stalks seems the perfect setting for the panda in this painting.

MATERIALS

SURFACE
10½" (27cm) basswood round from Walnut Hollow, supplied by Viking Woodcrafts, Inc.

BRUSHES
Robert Simmons Expression
no. 0 script liner
no. 2/0 liner
no. 3 round
no. 6 chisel blender
½" (12mm) flat
¾" (19mm) flat

Robert Simmons AquaTip
½" (12mm) oval wash

Loew-Cornell
18/0 short liner
⅛" (3mm) filbert rake
¼" (6mm) filbert rake

ADDITIONAL SUPPLIES
Delta Crackle Medium
Delta Matte Interior Spray Varnish
white chalk pencil or soapstone
Delta Matte Interior Varnish

DELTA CERAMCOAT ACRYLICS

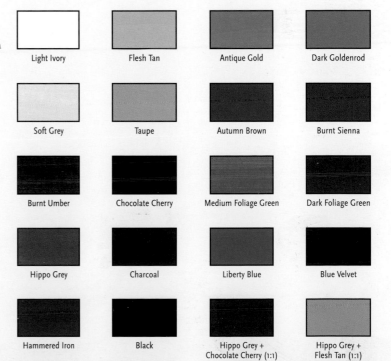

Light Ivory | Flesh Tan | Antique Gold | Dark Goldenrod
Soft Grey | Taupe | Autumn Brown | Burnt Sienna
Burnt Umber | Chocolate Cherry | Medium Foliage Green | Dark Foliage Green
Hippo Grey | Charcoal | Liberty Blue | Blue Velvet
Hammered Iron | Black | Hippo Grey + Chocolate Cherry (1:1) | Hippo Grey + Flesh Tan (1:1)
Taupe + Burnt Umber | Taupe + Burnt Umber + Medium Foliage Green | Taupe + Burnt Umber + Liberty Blue + Medium Foliage Green | Taupe + Burnt Umber + Liberty Blue

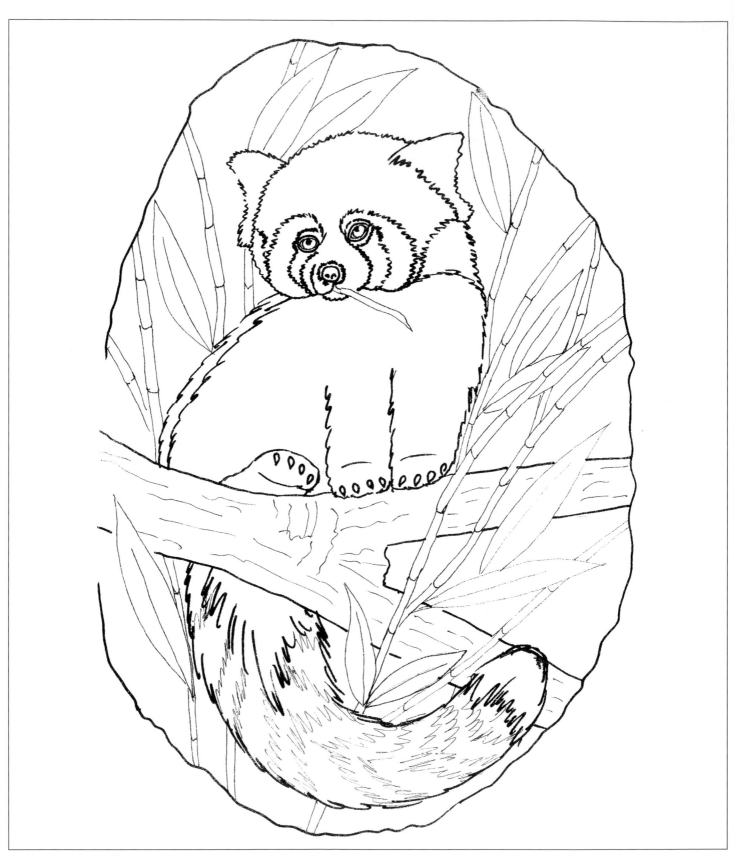

This pattern may be hand-traced or photocopied for personal use only.
Enlarge at 169 percent to bring it up to full size.

Faux Finish

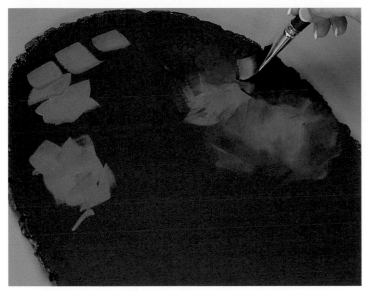

1 Sand the surface and seal, then sand again. Basecoat the entire surface with Dark Foliage Green on the ¾-inch (19mm) flat brush. With Medium Foliage Green on the same brush, paint splotches of color on the surface. Pick up some Dark Foliage Green on the brush and blend and soften the edges.

2 Wipe the brush with a paper towel, then pick up some Liberty Blue. Add splotches of this color and blend to soften the edges with more Dark Foliage Green.

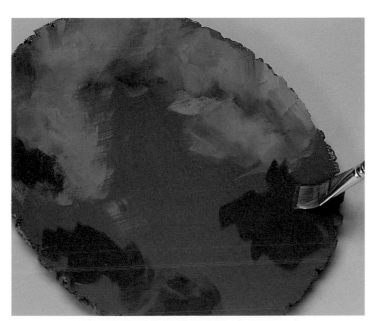

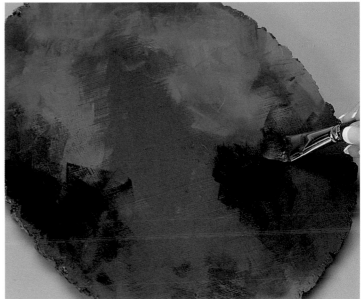

3 Wipe the brush and pick up Charcoal. Add this color in splotches, primarily to the lower portion of the surface, and soften the edges with a blend of Dark Foliage Green.

4 Wipe the brush and pick up Black and add it mostly to the bottom portion. Soften any hard edges with the Dark Foliage Green. Continue to add color and soften the edges, keeping lighter colors toward the top and darker colors toward the bottom.

Faux Finish, continued

5 Allow all paint colors to dry completely, then lightly spray two or three coats of matte spray to protect the background.

6 Transfer the pattern with white graphite paper and a stylus.

Crackled Branch

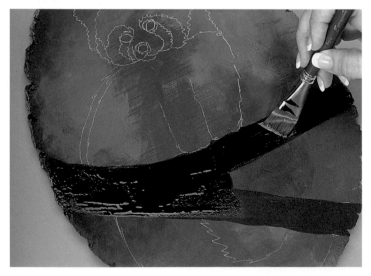

7 Basecoat the tree branch with Black using the ¾-inch (19mm) flat brush. When dry, apply a thin coat of crackle medium over the tree trunk and branches. Let set approximately 20 minutes, or according to the manufacturer's instructions.

8 Apply a very thin topcoat of Soft Grey with the ¾-inch (19mm) flat. Follow the grain of the wood, horizontally, until you get to the knot in the tree. Then switch directions and add some curved vertical strokes.

9 Wait for the crackle to dry completely, at least 24 hours, before continuing.

10 Basecoat the ears and muzzle with Antique Gold, the chest with Blue Velvet, the eyes and nose with Black and the head and back with Dark Goldenrod.

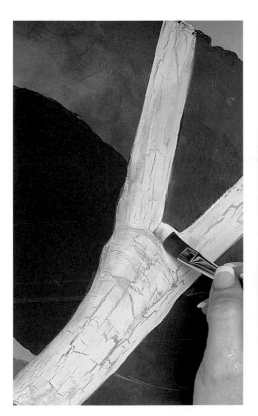

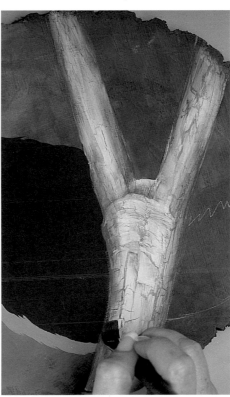

11 Thin a touch of Taupe with water to create a wash. Load the mix on the ¾-inch (19mm) flat and spread a thin coat over the branch. Let dry, then side load the ½-inch (12mm) oval wash with Autumn Brown. Float the Autumn Brown along the outside edges of the branch to help give it the appearance of roundness. Shade around some of the cracks to add interest to the interior of the branch.

12 Side load the wash brush with Charcoal and float this color over the Autumn Brown along the edges of the tree. Float the Charcoal only in areas that have been painted with Autumn Brown, not on the highlight areas.

Tail

13 Roughly basecoat the gold areas of the tail with Dark Goldenrod on the ½-inch (12mm) oval wash, using long, full strokes. Paint around the base and tip of the tail since these areas will be Blue Velvet. Follow the directional flow diagram.

14 Load a no. 3 round brush with Blue Velvet thinned with just enough water to make the paint move. Basecoat the dark patches at the base and tip of the tail. Pull the strokes in toward the Dark Goldenrod.

Fur Directional Flow

15 Transfer the pattern details onto the panda with white graphite paper and a stylus. With a white chalk pencil or soapstone, draw in the directional flow of the fur so that you have a directional reference when you begin to pull the fur strokes.

Face Floats

16 Side load the ½-inch (12mm) wash brush with Hammered Iron and paint a flip-float with the loaded edge in the center of ear. Load the brush with Blue Velvet and shade a smaller flip-float within the area shaded with Hammered Iron.

17 Side load Hammered Iron onto the no. 6 chisel blender. Float the color around the top of the eyes, around the nose and below the mouth.

Brown Fur

18 Load the ¼-inch (6mm) filbert rake with inky Burnt Sienna, as described on page 12. Stroke in the long hairs of the tail in the striped area. Lift the brush at the end of each long stroke to give the appearance of soft fur.

19 With inky Burnt Sienna, stroke in hairs in the gold area around the nose. Tap the brush for these tiny hairs. As you move further from the nose, paint the hairs slightly longer. In the gold areas on the red panda's cheeks, paint more strokes with the Burnt Sienna to make this area darker.

Brown Fur, continued

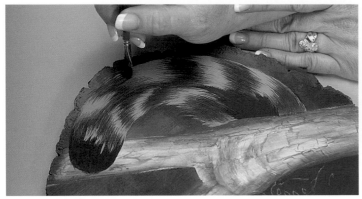

20 Load the ¼-inch (6mm) filbert rake with inky Chocolate Cherry and fill in the centers of the Burnt Sienna stripes on the tail. Begin to color weave by stroking the Chocolate Cherry into the neighboring colors both above and below the stripes.

21 Add inky Chocolate Cherry over some of the Burnt Sienna areas on the face to darken them. Darken the top of the head to make it appear to curve back. Create a few dark tufts on the forehead and continue to darken the cheeks.

22 Load the filbert rake with inky Antique Gold and start to build highlights in the Dark Goldenrod areas of the tail. Pull the strokes into the dark stripes above and below the one you are working on. Allow some of the Dark Goldenrod to show through.

23 Begin to build highlights on the head by stroking inky Antique Gold in the gold areas where you did not use Chocolate Cherry. Since these areas are closer to the nose, pounce short tiny strokes instead of stroking long ones.

24 Stroke in the lightest highlights on the tail with inky Flesh Tan. Place these in small areas within the Antique Gold so that you can see every color you have used so far.

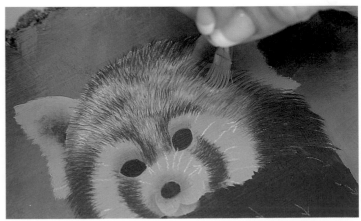

25 Add a few inky Flesh Tan highlights over some of the Antique Gold on the face.

White Fur

26 Stroke inky Flesh Tan into the white areas on the face. Use either the ⅛-inch (3mm) or ¼-inch (6mm) filbert rake brush, whichever is more comfortable for working in these small areas. Remember to keep the hair closest to the nose very short.

27 Clean the brush and load with inky Light Ivory. Add these strokes to the middle of the Flesh Tan areas for the lightest hairs in the white areas.

Claws

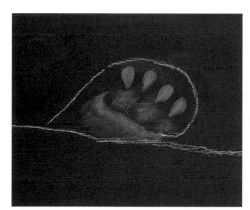

28 Load the no. 2/0 liner with Hippo Grey and stroke in a base coat for the nails. For the up-turned paw, side load the no. 6 chisel blender with Hippo Grey and paint flip-floats for the pads of the paw.

29 Shade under the nails with Black side loaded on the chisel blender. Then brush-mix Hippo Grey and Flesh Tan (1:1) and load onto the 18/0 liner. Start near the center of the nail, and paint a short line toward the end of the nail for the highlight. Stroke in the fur with Hippo Grey on the ¼-inch (6mm) filbert rake.

30 Side load the no. 6 chisel blender with Blue Velvet and paint a small C-stroke at the top of each nail to shade.

Fur on Chest

31 Load the ¼-inch (6mm) filbert rake with inky Hippo Grey and fill in a little bit of fur on the chest, going down the legs and around the edges of the chest.

32 Load the ¼-inch (6mm) filbert rake with Chocolate Cherry and pull fur strokes onto the rest of the chest and legs. Brush-mix Hippo Grey and Chocolate Cherry (1:1), and load this onto the same brush. Brush this over the straight Chocolate Cherry strokes to highlight just the ends of some of these dark hairs.

Eyes

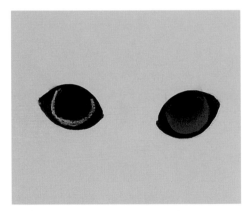 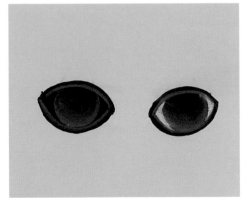 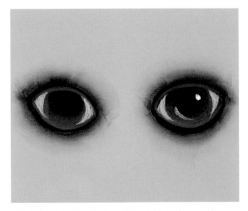

33 Transfer the pattern for the irises to the surface with white graphite paper and a stylus (shown on the animal's right eye above).

Side load Autumn Brown onto the no. 6 chisel blender and paint a C-stroke on the iris line (shown on the animal's left eye).

34 Thin Hippo Grey and load on the 18/0 liner, then outline each eye slightly inside the dark base coat (shown on the right eye).

Load the chisel blender with Flesh Tan and fill in the corners of the eyes (shown on the left eye).

35 Side load the chisel blender with Black and shade around the entire eye with the color side of the brush toward the eye (shown on the right eye).

Load the 18/0 liner with Light Ivory and highlight each eye with a comma stroke in the lower left part of the eye. Tap a sparkle dot of Light Ivory into the upper right part of each iris (shown on the left eye).

Nose and Color Weaving

36 Basecoat the nose Black. Transfer the nostril pattern to the surface when dry. Side load the no. 6 chisel blender with Hippo Grey and tap the loaded side above the nostrils. Flip the brush over and blend the color between the nostrils. Side load the brush with Black and float it around the nose onto the muzzle.

With the same brush, place a Black float around the paws and down the sides of the legs.

Color weave the fur all over the body, using each of the colors you have already used until the red panda looks soft and fluffy. Refer to pages 72-74 for color-weaving techniques.

Foliage

37 Place the background colors plus Taupe separately on your palette. Basecoat the parts of the bamboo and leaves that overlap the branch. The goal for the background is subtle contrast, so basecoat with colors that are just a step up or down from the dominant color in the area you are working in. For example, at the bottom of the piece use Medium Foliage Green plus Charcoal to basecoat the leaf because there is a lot of Charcoal in that area. With Medium Foliage Green and a touch of Charcoal, paint the stick in the mouth. If you cannot see what you are painting, add a slightly brighter color. If it is too bright, tone it down with a touch more Charcoal.

38 Side load the ½-inch (12mm) flat with mixtures of Dark Foliage Green and Charcoal. Run the chisel end down one side of the bamboo shoots, then round up, like a C, to create the segment for the bamboo. If you wish, draw in the segment lines of the bamboo sticks, placing these lines every inch or so.

Foliage, continued

39 Shade the leaves using colors from the background, with a side-loaded ½-inch (12mm) flat. Float the color down one side of each leaf and then down the center, without flipping the brush. If you wish, draw in the center line of the leaves before painting these floats.

40 For the highlights, use various combinations of the following colors, depending on where you are working in the painting: Medium Foliage Green, Liberty Blue, and a combination of Taupe and Burnt Umber. Side load the ½-inch (12mm) flat and highlight the sides of each leaf opposite the shading. On the bamboo stalks, float the color along the top of each segment and down the side opposite the shading.

Whiskers

41 Side load the chisel edge of the flat brush with one of the highlight colors and pull a light line down the shaft of each segment of the bamboo to give it roundness.

42 With the no. 0 script liner and inky Light Ivory, delicately paint in the whiskers using just the tip of the brush.

43 Erase any remaining graphite lines, then sign and date your piece. Apply several coats of brush-on matte varnish to protect your painting.

Baby Bobcats

These cute little kittens have played themselves out and are in need of a long nap. Cuddled up together for warmth and comfort, sleep should come quickly.

Big blue eyes mark the central focus of this painting; very soft fur and intertwining body parts are also key. When painting this fur, use a very light touch for the fine hairs with a very dense undercoat. The black markings are strong but have softened edges moving into the brown areas.

The faux-finished background should be coarse and choppy to create an interesting texture that the natural bark edges of the basswood plank will perfectly complete.

MATERIALS

SURFACE

13" (33cm) basswood plank from Walnut Hollow, supplied by Viking Woodcrafts, Inc.

BRUSHES

Robert Simmons Expression

no. 2/0 round
no. 3 round
⅛" (3mm) angle shader
⅜" (10mm) angle shader
¾" (19mm) angle shader
¾" (19mm) flat

Robert Simmons AquaTip

½" (12mm) oval mop

Loew-Cornell

18/0 short liner
¼" (6mm) filbert rake

ADDITIONAL SUPPLIES

upholstery foam cut in small
    pieces
Delta Crackle Medium
Delta Matte Interior Varnish

DELTA CERAMCOAT ACRYLICS

White	Wild Rice	Putty	Dunes Beige
Bambi Brown	Lichen Grey	Coral	Burnt Sienna
Burnt Umber	Williamsburg Blue	Hippo Grey	Black Green

| Black | Williamsburg Blue + White (1:1) |

This pattern may be hand-traced or photocopied for personal use only.
Enlarge at 133 percent to bring up to full size.

Background

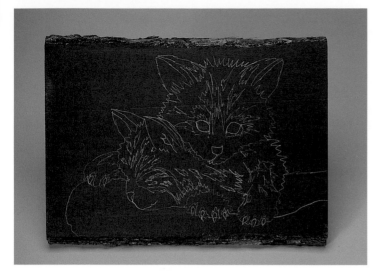

1 Sand the surface, then seal with wood sealer. Lightly sand again. Basecoat the surface with Black Green using the ¾-inch flat brush. Lightly transfer the pattern onto the surface with white graphite paper and a stylus.

2 Cut at least three pieces of upholstery foam that are approximately 1" x 1" x 2" (2.5cm x 2.5cm x 5cm). Dip one foam block into Black Green and make slip-slap Xs randomly in the background around the bobcats, leaving some spots uncovered. Overlap the edges of the pattern a bit with the color. While the paint is still wet, load a clean piece of foam with Hippo Grey and fill in Xs between the Black Green Xs.

Crackle on Log

3 Using a clean piece of foam, slightly blend the edges where the gray and black-green areas meet. Do not overblend and lose the color variation; you want this to look rough and choppy.

4 With the ¾-inch (19mm) flat, apply a fairly heavy coat of crackle medium, spreading it as thick as icing on a cake. Let set until partially dry; follow the directions on the bottle for specific instructions for that product.

Log

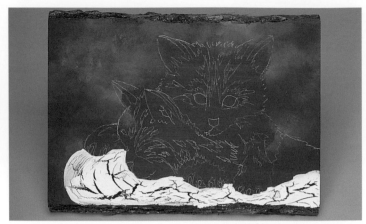

5 Overstroke the crackle medium with a medium to heavy coat of White. Stroke on the White paint in the direction you'd like the cracks to run. For deep cracks like these, apply the overcoat when crackle medium is less dry and use more paint.

6 The white paint will continue to crack until it dries completely. Do not attempt to adjust this area once the paint begins to crack and while it is still wet. If adjustments are needed, wait at least 24 hours, then work on it until you're satisfied with the result.

7 Using the ¾-inch(19mm) angle shader, mix a wash of mostly water and a touch of Burnt Sienna on your palette paper. Blot out the extra mix in your brush on a paper towel. Reload the brush with the wash. Brush it randomly on the log.

8 Make a wash with Burnt Umber and repeat the previous step, creating shadows on the fallen log.

9 Side load the ¾-inch (19mm) angle shader with Hippo Grey. With rough and choppy strokes, deepen the shadow areas around the edge of the log and under the bobcats. Also float the color around some of the more interesting cracks to deepen them.

10 Load the brush with Black and again shade under the bobcats, around the log and around a few of the cracks.

Base Coat for Fur

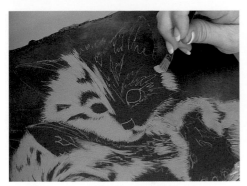

11 Load the ¼-inch (6mm) filbert rake with Bambi Brown, thinned just enough so the paint can move. Stroke in the fur, closely following the directional flow diagram. Leave some of the background showing through and work around the black spots on the pattern. Refer to the finished photograph on page 111, too, if this helps. If you paint over a black spot, you can always add it back in later.

12 As you are basecoating, begin to color weave the Bambi Brown into the areas you are leaving black.

13 Pay particular attention to the front paw as you are basecoating. The directional flow of the fur should come out in all directions from a point near the top of the paw.

Fur Directional Flow

14 Complete the basecoating. Place the pattern over the base coat to make sure the black spots are still intact; adjust as necessary.

Fur

15 Mix Dunes Beige to an inky consistency with the ¼-inch (6mm) filbert rake brush. Blot the brush on a paper towel, then load as described on page 12. Paint short strokes of fur on the bobcats, following the directional flow diagram. It can be helpful to place a few strokes of fur here and there so that you do not lose track of the ever-changing direction of the fur as you paint in the different areas.

16 Finish stroking in the Dunes Beige, including along the edges of the ears. Do not cover all the Bambi Brown fur because the more colors you can see, the denser the fur will appear.

17 Before continuing with the fur, side load the ½-inch (12mm) oval mop with Coral and apply a heavy float inside each ear, keeping the loaded side up against the black rim.

18 Load the ¼-inch (6mm) filbert rake with inky Wild Rice and stroke fur into the lighter areas around the eyes, muzzles and the edges of the ears. To paint fur in the narrow area around eyes and between black spots, place the brush on its narrow chisel edge and pull straight back. As you get to a wider area, turn the brush and start making strokes with the full width again.

Claws

19 Clean the brush and load with inky Hippo Grey. Referring to the finished photograph on page 111, place the Hippo Grey in the darkest areas of light fur and randomly on the medium fur. This subtle gradation of color gives the bobcats depth.

20 Load the no. 2/0 round with Lichen Grey. Basecoat the nails by painting two interlocking comma strokes, one to the left and one to the right.

Fur, continued

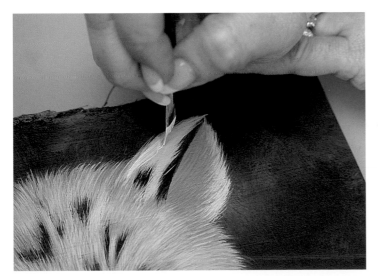

21 Load the ¼-inch (6mm) filbert rake with inky Putty and lighten the lightest areas of fur.

22 Continue to add Putty in the lightest areas until you are satisfied with the result. Basecoat the noses with Coral using the no. 3 round. When dry, draw or transfer lines for the nostrils. (The nostrils will be completed in step 28.)

Fur, continued

23 Side load the ¾-inch (19mm) angle shader with Hippo Grey. Shade around the outside edges of the cats, using a zigzag motion with the chisel edge of the brush to keep the appearance of fur. Deepen the shadows between the cats to separate them. Shade the small black spots with Hippo Grey using the ⅜-inch (10mm) angle shader. Keep the chisel edge running in the direction of the fur.

24 Begin to color weave with the Hippo Grey, pulling the fur down from the black spots into the area below.

Feet

25 Load the ⅜-inch (10mm) angle shader with Black and reinforce the shading you applied with Hippo Grey. This shading should be smaller than the previous float. There should be a glow of Hippo Grey all around each black spot. As with the Hippo Grey, pull a few strokes down to color weave in the area below the shading. Keep the strokes running in the direction of the directional flow diagram.

26 With the ⅜-inch (10mm) angle shader, shade the fur around each claw with Hippo Grey and then Black to give them depth.

27 Side load the ⅛-inch (3mm) angle shader with Hippo Grey and shade on the right side of the inside of each claw. With a side load of Wild Rice, tap a highlight in the medium value area of each claw.

Noses

28 Using the ⅛-inch (3mm) angle shader loaded with Black, shade on the inside of each nose, following the nostril lines you drew, then shade around the outside of the noses. Extend the outside float slightly beyond the top of the nose.

29 Extend the lines from each eye toward the nose with the same brush.

Eyes

30 Place the pattern over the eyes to check the accuracy of the shapes, and basecoat with Black on the no. 3 round. When dry, sketch or transfer the iris and pupil.

31 Basecoat the iris with Williamsburg Blue using the no. 3 round. Then mix Williamsburg Blue and White (1:1) and paint a flip-float on the bottom of the iris (shown on the animal's left eye).

32 Mix Black and water to an inky consistency with the 18/0 liner. Pull small lines radiating from the pupil into the iris. First pull the strokes where the numbers on a clock would be (shown here on the animal's left eye), then fill the spaces between the strokes with more small lines (shown on the right eye).

33 Use the liner brush to reinforce the Black line around the top of the iris. Side load the ⅛-inch (3mm) angle shader with Black and shade across the top of the eye (shown on the left eye).

34 Side load the ⅛-inch (3mm) angle shader with White and float a highlight in the upper area of the eye, but do not cover all of the black of the pupil.

35 Reload the brush with more White, then tap a sparkle in the center of the highlight. Dab a little highlight in the iris of each eye.

36 Make any final adjustments, and then color weave the fur as described in project five, pages 72-74. Using the 18/0 liner loaded with inky Lichen Grey, pull strokes to create the whiskers. Repeat lightly with Putty. Sign and date your piece. When dry, varnish with several thin, even coats of brush-on matte varnish.

Autumn Red Fox

This beautiful fox just draws you in with its piercing eyes. Getting the shape and form of the animal's facial structure can be challenging as well as rewarding. Remember that there is a skull under all that beautiful fur. This will help you create the eye sockets that are set back in the head and the brow and muzzle that come forward. Color weaving will create many different tones and hues, even within the same color fur. It also gives the fox a beautiful red glow.

Surrounding the fox with autumn leaves is the perfect finishing touch for this painting. Keep the leaves subtle; it ensures that the fox remains the focus of the painting.

MATERIALS

SURFACE
10½" (27cm) basswood round from Walnut Hollow, supplied by Viking Woodcrafts, Inc.

BRUSHES
Robert Simmons Expression
no. 0 script liner
no. 3 round
no. 6 round
½" (12mm) angle shader
no. 6 chisel blender
no. 12 flat
¾" (19mm) flat

Robert Simmons Fabric Mate
no. 6 fabric scrubber

Robert Simmons AquaTip
½" (12mm) oval wash
¾" (19mm) oval wash

Loew-Cornell
18/0 short liner
¼" (6mm) filbert rake

ADDITIONAL SUPPLIES
Delta Gel Blending Medium
Delta Matte Interior Spray Varnish
soapstone or white chalk pencil
Delta Matte Interior Varnish

DELTA CERAMCOAT ACRYLICS

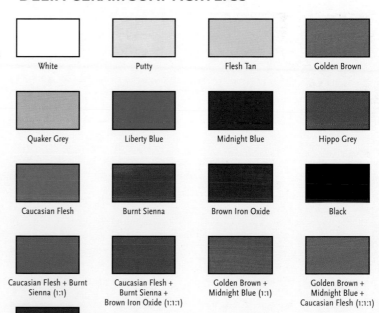

White	Putty	Flesh Tan	Golden Brown
Quaker Grey	Liberty Blue	Midnight Blue	Hippo Grey
Caucasian Flesh	Burnt Sienna	Brown Iron Oxide	Black
Caucasian Flesh + Burnt Sienna (1:1)	Caucasian Flesh + Burnt Sienna + Brown Iron Oxide (1:1:1)	Golden Brown + Midnight Blue (1:1)	Golden Brown + Midnight Blue + Caucasian Flesh (1:1:1)
Midnight Blue + touch of Golden Brown			

This pattern may
be hand-traced or
photocopied for
personal use only.
Enlarge at 179
percent to bring up
to full size.

Background and Base Coat

1 Sand the basswood round and seal it with wood sealer, then sand again. Basecoat the surface with Liberty Blue using the ¾-inch (19mm) flat brush. Allow to dry and, if needed, apply a second base coat for full coverage. When dry, transfer the outline of the fox onto the surface with white graphite paper and a stylus.

Load the ¾-inch (19mm) oval wash brush with blending gel, then with Liberty Blue, and apply the mixture around and up to the fox pattern. Load the brush with more blending gel and a touch of Midnight Blue. Place this color around the outside edge where there should be no freshly painted Liberty Blue. Wipe your brush with a clean paper towel, then begin blending the colors with a slip-slap motion and a very light touch. Periodically wipe the brush on a paper towel. Add more blending gel to the brush if the blend on the surface starts to drag.

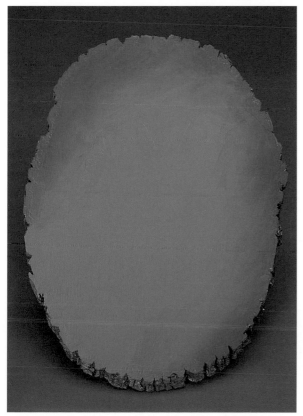

2 Continue blending in this fashion, reloading the brush as needed until the rest of the edge of the surface is finished and the blending is smooth. Continue to wipe the brush and add blending gel as needed. Let dry thoroughly, then spray with two or three light coats of matte spray to protect the faux finish.

3 Transfer the color breaks shown on the pattern to the wood piece. Basecoat the ears, cheeks and the light spot on the shoulder with Golden Brown. Base the head and back with Caucasian Flesh and the chest with Hippo Grey. Base the legs of the fox with Brown Iron Oxide. Basecoat the eyes and nose with Black.

Tip

Each basswood oval will be shaped differently as these are slices of actual trees. They will vary in size and shape—sometimes a lot. You may need to adjust the placement of the animal or background elements to suit your individual piece.

Ears

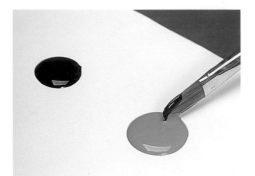

4 To double load the ½-inch (12mm) oval wash brush, dip one corner of the brush in Black, then dip the other in Golden Brown. Keep the handle parallel to the palette so the paint does not go too far across the brush.

5 With the brush handle straight up and down, apply pressure to blend the colors together where they meet.

6 Reload the colors on the brush. Flip the brush and blend the other side. Repeat this two or three times for a full brush and a smooth gradation of color from Golden Brown on one end to Black on the other.

7 To begin to create the inside of the ear, pat the double-loaded brush at the base with Black toward the middle. Pat the brush to the top of the ear, narrowing the application to match the overall shape of the ear. It is always easier to pull the stroke toward you, so turn the piece upside down.

8 Flip the brush over, so the Black side of the brush touches the Black part of the first stroke. Then pat the brush on the other side of the same ear. Make sure the application is wider at the base of the ear and narrower at the top. Reload the brush and repeat for the other ear.

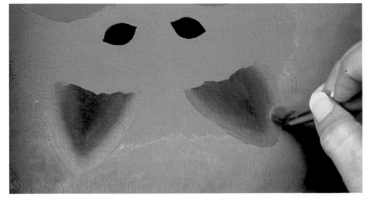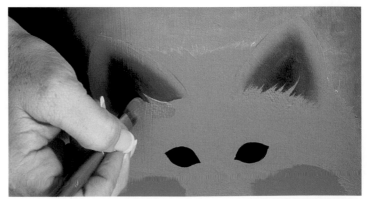

9 Side load the same brush with Caucasian Flesh and float the color down the outside edges of each ear.

10 With the chisel edge of the ½-inch (12mm) oval mop brush, pull a few strokes of Caucasian Flesh from the base coat into the ear to break the hard edge of the Black.

Fur

11 With a soapstone or white chalk pencil, draw the fur direction lines on the surface so that you can easily follow the flow while you are painting.

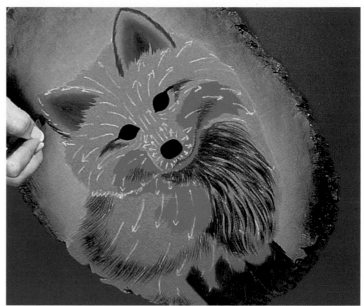

12 Thin a puddle of Black paint with water (1:1) to achieve an inky consistency. Load the ¼-inch (6mm) filbert rake brush as described on page 12. Roughly paint Black hair strokes in the darkest fur areas on the face, cheeks, body and chest. Pull the fur on the legs with a lighter touch. For the ears, use the chisel edge of the brush and paint short strokes along the outside edges of both ears.

Fur Directional Flow

13 Load the filbert rake brush with inky Flesh Tan and begin to build the light fur in the areas basecoated with Golden Brown. For the ears, start at the base, pull long strokes and work toward the tip with shorter strokes. Again use the chisel edge of the brush to pull short strokes on the outside edge of the ears, next to the black rim.

Please Note

Due to technical difficulties, the colors in steps 9 through 23 of this project are not accurate. Please follow the captions for the colors used to paint these steps.

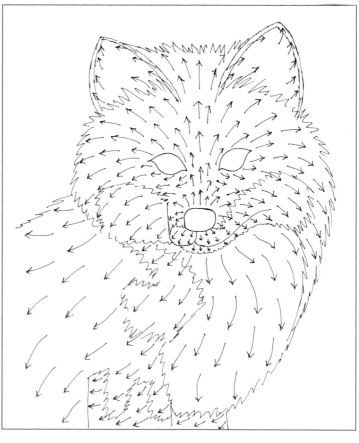

Fur, continued

14 Load the ¼-inch (6mm) filbert rake, as before, with inky Brown Iron Oxide, and pull fur strokes on the Caucasian Flesh areas. Make sure the fur strokes get shorter as they get closer to the nose.

15 With Burnt Sienna loaded on the filbert rake, add more strokes of color in the brown areas—this brightens the brown areas.

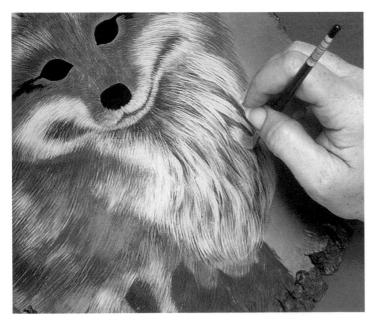

16 Load the same brush with inky Quaker Grey and build lighter fur onto the chest. Layer the fur, but be sure it looks natural, not like it has been combed. Add a few larger tufts of fur that gently cross the flow of the fur. Pull a few strokes of Quaker Grey over the black areas of the cheeks to soften this darker fur.

17 Load the brush again, this time with inky Putty and over-stroke highlights in the light areas of fur on the shoulder and cheeks. For the ears, paint some short strokes at the tips and around the edges, but also paint in some longer tufts with the edge of the brush (as done on the chest). Lighten the chest slightly with a few strokes of Putty.

18 All the fur is placed now, but it is still very coarse. So you will need to color weave to get the soft, natural look of real fur. Remember, color weaving takes a bit of time, so if you would like to take a break from fur, you may want to skip to the eyes and nose, then do the color weaving. (See pages 72–74 for color-weaving techniques.)

Color Weaving

19 Place puddles of Caucasian Flesh, Burnt Sienna, Brown Iron Oxide, Flesh Tan and Putty on your palette. Mix each color separately with water (1:1) to an inky consistency. Load one color at a time on the filbert rake and weave each color into the neighboring color as described in project five. Remember, the key is to keep the pressure off the brush so the fur is light and fluffy. The pressure should be much lighter than was used in the previous steps.

20 Side load the ¾-inch (19mm) flat brush with Black and float it under the chin to separate the head from the body. If necessary to anchor the nose to the face, side load the brush with Brown Iron Oxide and float it around the nose.

Eyes

21 Side load the no. 12 flat brush with Brown Iron Oxide and float a C-stroke for the iris, leaving a narrow rim of the Black base coat at the bottom. Let this dry. Side load the same brush with Golden Brown and apply a slightly narrower C-stroke over the previous stroke. Allow this to dry completely, then lightly sketch in the pupil with your soapstone or white chalk pencil.

22 Side load the no. 6 chisel blender with Golden Brown and highlight the iris with a small float in the middle of the iris. Flip the brush to create a back-to-back highlight. With the same brush, float Black in for the pupil with the loaded edge against the line you drew in.

23 Load the 18/0 liner brush with inky Black. Set the brush in the pupil, then pull thin lines out into the iris, varying the length of the lines. First place the lines at the numbers on a clock face, then fill in with more lines to break the hard edge of the pupil.

24 Load the 18/0 liner the same way, consecutively, with inky Brown Iron Oxide, inky Burnt Sienna and then inky Golden Brown. Place these lines in between the Black lines radiating into the iris. Pull Golden Brown lines mainly through the iris highlight in the bottom center of the eye.

25 Side load the no. 12 flat with Black and float a shadow under the entire eyelid of each eye. Side load the no. 6 chisel blender with Putty and float a highlight C-stroke in the upper right of each eye and a little highlight in the lower left corner. Load the chisel blender with White and tap a tiny sparkle in each Putty highlight; angle the top highlight toward the bottom highlight. Side load the chisel blender with Black and float down the inside corner of each eye to set them into the head.

Nose

26 Sketch the nostrils with a soapstone, placing the top of the nostrils at the halfway point of the nose. Notice that the nostrils are flat on top, not round.

27 Side load the no. 6 chisel blender with Hippo Grey and roughly float a highlight straight across the nose. Flip the brush and float the color between the nostrils.

28 With Black, re-establish the shape of the nostrils, if needed. Side load a tiny bit of White on the chisel blender and tap the color into the Hippo Grey highlight, going straight across the nose. Reload the brush with White and repeat the stroke in a much smaller area for a sparkle.

Final Fur Adjustment

29 Load the no. 12 flat brush with a mix of mostly water and a touch of Burnt Sienna. Brush this wash over the red-brown areas of the fox to give it a richer red tint. Let dry, then apply multiple washes if you would like your fox to have an even redder tint.

Whiskers

30 Before applying whiskers, be sure you are happy with your color weaving; if not, add more. If you wish, preserve your painting with a few light coats of matte spray before you apply the whiskers. Then you will not have to worry about damaging the fur if you remove and redo the whiskers.

With your soapstone, roughly sketch in some whisker guides, starting them in the white area below the nose and pulling them out with a slight arc. Load the no. 0 script liner with inky Hippo Grey. Keeping the brush handle straight up and down, apply a little pressure at the base of the whisker and gradually release pressure as you pull out to the ends. Do not try to follow the lines exactly; just use them as a guide. Following too closely may make the whiskers look stiff.

31 Deepen the color on some whiskers with an inky brush mix of Hippo Grey and Black. To make it look like the whiskers are growing from under the fur, lightly tap a bit of Putty over the base of each whisker.

Leaves

32 Transfer the patterns for the leaves, adjusting them as necessary to fit your surface. Remember they are leaves, so they can vary in size and shape. Place separate puddles of Caucasian Flesh, Golden Brown, Burnt Sienna, Brown Iron Oxide and Midnight Blue onto your palette. For the brown leaves, mix varying amounts of Caucasian Flesh and Burnt Sienna with a touch of water. Loosely basecoat the leaves with the no. 6 round brush. Some of the background will show through, and the base coat need not be smooth in coverage. Pick up a little Brown Iron Oxide on the dirty brush and basecoat the darker brown leaves. Base the green leaves with a mix of varying amounts of Golden Brown and Midnight Blue. Play with creating a variety of fall-colored leaves. Do not be restricted by the pattern!

Draw in the center and side veins with a soapstone.

Scrub Golden Brown and Caucasian Flesh in between the veins for a highlight.

33 Load the no. 3 round brush with Golden Brown and wiggle in a couple of stems between the leaves. Leave the paint slightly watery so it is transparent. With your soapstone, sketch in the center and side vein lines on the leaves. Dip a dry no. 6 fabric scrubber in the Golden Brown and work the brush in a circular motion on your palette to get the paint into the bristles. Scrub the paint in between the vein lines on some of the leaves. Pick up some Caucasian Flesh on the dirty brush and highlight a few more leaves. Adjust the colors as necessary and desired for the leaf colors.

Shade the leaves with Burnt Sienna and Midnight Blue.

Darken the shading further with Brown Iron Oxide and Midnight Blue.

Streak Midnight Blue on the leaves, then float it around the edges of the leaves.

34 For all the brown leaves, side load the ½-inch (12mm) angle shader with Burnt Sienna and float the first shade along one side of the center vein. Start at the base of the leaf with a wider float and narrow it to the tip of the leaf. Flip the brush over and float the shade on the other side of the leaf, leaving a narrow line of background color in the center to create the vein. Repeat with a narrower float of Brown Iron Oxide to darken the center vein. Using a very narrow side load of Burnt Sienna, Brown Iron Oxide or a mix with Midnight Blue, paint the smaller side veins. These come off the wider center vein in a very slight S shape. Float a few Midnight Blue leaves on the blue background to suggest leaves further in the background.

35 Load the no. 12 flat with mostly water and a touch of Midnight Blue. Blot the loaded brush on a paper towel. Beginning at the outside edges of a few leaves, streak the color remaining on the brush on the leaves, pulling and lifting the brush in the direction of the side veins. Mix a little Golden Brown with the blue on the dirty brush to vary the color for other leaves. Apply some streaking on each leaf, but vary the colors to create a more interesting overall effect.

Load the ¾-inch (19mm) flat with thinned Midnight Blue and float the color along the edge of the board wherever the leaves touch the edge. Where the fox touches the edge of the board, float Brown Iron Oxide.

36 Erase any remaining graphite or soapstone lines. Sign and date your piece, then varnish with several thin coats of brush-on matte varnish.

RESOURCES

Paints

Delta Ceramcoat
2550 Pellissier Place
Whittier, CA 90601
(800) 423-4135
www.deltacrafts.com

Brushes

Daler-Rowney
Robert Simmons Expression
2 Corporate Dr.
Cranbury, NJ 08512
(609) 655-5252
fax (609) 655-5852

Loew-Cornell, Inc.
563 Chestnut Ave.
Teaneck, NJ 07666
(201) 836-7070

Surfaces

Valhalla Designs
343 Twin Pines Dr.
Glendale, OR 97442
(541) 832-3260
e-mail: valhalla@mcsi.net

Viking Woodcrafts, Inc.
1317 8th St. S.E.
Waseca, MN 56093
(800) 461-5888
fax: (507) 835-3895
www.vikingwoodcrafts.com

General Supplies

The Painter's Palette
Decorative Arts Studio
2980 McClintock Way no. F
Costa Mesa, CA 92626
(714) 432-8653
fax (714) 432-8658

Viking Woodcrafts, Inc.
see under Surfaces

Canadian Retailers

Crafts Canada
2745 29th St. N.E.
Calgary, ON, T1Y 7B5

MacPherson Craft Wholesale
83 Queen St. E.
P.O. Box 1870
St. Mary's, ON, N4X 1C2
(519) 284-1741

Mercury Art & Craft Supershop
332 Wellington St.
London, ON, N6C 4P7
(519) 434-1636

Town & Country
Folk Art Supplies
93 Green Lane
Thornhill, ON, L3T 6K6
(905) 882-0199

INDEX

EXPLORE THE WORLD OF DECORATIVE PAINTING WITH NORTH LIGHT BOOKS!

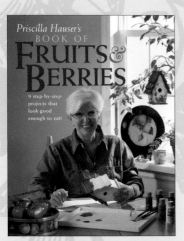

Painting fruits and berries is easy with the help of Priscilla Hauser, the "first lady" of decorative painting. She shows you how to capture the colors and textures of all your favorites, including holly, pine sprigs, mistletoe, lemons, strawberries, pears, plums, blackberries and apples.

Nine heavily illustrated step-by-step projects will teach you how to paint fruits and berries on everything from tin canisters and bowls to wheelbarrows, candles and more!

1-58180-070-3, paperback, 128 pages

Learn to paint your favorite Christmas themes, including Santas, angels, elves and more, on everything from glittering ornaments to festive albums with these nine all-new, step-by-step projects from renowned decorative painter, John Gutcher.

He makes mastering those tricky details simple with special tips for painting fur, hair, richly textured clothing and realistic flesh tones. Just follow along with John to create a range of wonderful holiday heirlooms!

1-58180-105-X, paperback, 128 pages

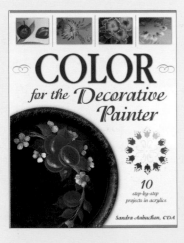

This guide makes using color simple. Best of all, it's as fun as it is instructional, featuring ten step-by-step projects that illustrate color principles in action.

As you paint your favorite subjects—be they flowers, fruit or birds—you'll learn how to make color work for you. No second-guessing, no regrets, just great-looking paintings and a whole lot of pleasure.

1-58180-048-7, paperback, 128 pages

Learn to paint miniature decorative painting masterpieces with these 14 full-color, step-by-step projects, including Victorian vanity boxes, wooden nesting dolls, holiday ornaments and more.

All the instructions are supplemented with hints and sidebars, complete materials lists, color palettes and designs ready to be hand traced or photocopied. A glossary of terms and techniques completes the package so that you'll never be without guidance.

0-89134-992-8, paperback, 128 pages